MORAL VALUES AND POLITICAL BEHAVIOUR IN ANCIENT GREECE

From Homer to the end of the Fifth Century

ANCIENT CULTURE AND SOCIETY

General Editor
M. I. FINLEY
Professor of Ancient History
at the University of Cambridge

Other titles in preparation

MORAL VALUES AND POLITICAL BEHAVIOUR IN ANCIENT GREECE

From Homer to the end of the Fifth Century

A. W. H. ADKINS
Professor of Classics, University of Reading

W · W · NORTON & COMPANY · INC · NEW YORK

Library of Congress Cataloging in Publication Data
Adkins, Arthur W H
  Moral values and political behaviour in ancient
Greece.
    (Ancient culture and society)
    Bibliography: p
    I. Ethics, Greek.   I. Title.
BJ182.A3 1973   172   72–8796
ISBN 0–393–04367–3

Printed in the United States of America

1 2 3 4 5 6 7 8 9 0

CONTENTS

PREFACE

THOUGH the number of those who can read Greek texts in the original language declines, interest in ancient Greece becomes ever more widespread; and the number of Greekless students of ancient Greek values and political behaviour, the subject of the present work, is now very large indeed. In writing this book, I have endeavoured to make it accessible to the Greekless reader, and have accordingly translated the texts on which the discussion is based. However, for reasons which are set out in the first chapter, the most important Greek terms of value are untranslatable; and any real understanding of Greek values and society must be based on detailed observation of the behaviour of these terms. Consequently, the key terms—a small group, but one whose members appear on virtually every page of Greek—are not translated but transliterated. I am, of course, aware that it is more difficult for the Greekless reader to read a book of this nature than one which uses English words throughout; but I would contend, and hope that Greekless readers will agree, that some of the points that I am trying to make here could only be made at much greater length, while others—and those some of the most important—could not be made at all, if this method were not used.

This work evidently has some relationship to my *Merit and Responsibility* (Clarendon 1960), and acknowledges the same debts as that work, notably to Professor E. R. Dodds and Professor B. Snell, whose thought has ever served as a guide and stimulus to my own. However, the scope and emphasis of this book are different: in *Merit and Responsibility* I was principally concerned with situations of crisis, where competitive and co-operative excellences are in conflict; in this work I have devoted more space to discussing co-operative excellences in their own right, with the result that a number of topics are discussed here that do not appear at all in the earlier work.

It gives me great pleasure to be able to thank here Cornell

PREFACE

University, the Society for the Humanities and its Director, Professor Max Black, for the research opportunities which I enjoyed during the academic year 1969–70 as a Senior Visiting Fellow of that most humane and welcoming of institutions, in which the period of reading and gestation required by this work was spent in conditions ideal for the purpose; and also to thank Professor M. I. Finley and Mr. John Roberts, each of whom read this work in typescript and made numerous comments for which both my readers and I have reason to be grateful. My thanks are due also to Mrs. D. Janes and Mrs. A. G. Conner, who divined the sense of my longhand and translated it into elegant typescript.

Note on Transliteration

A few words are needed to explain my transliterations. These are direct: each Greek letter is represented by its equivalent in the Roman alphabet, whether or no the pronunciation of the letter coincides with that of the Greek, save that double gamma is rendered by 'ng'. In general, I have marked long vowels on the first occasion of a word's appearance, and in the index. Short vowels are not marked at all, except in the case of words like *aischĕă* (p. 31), where the Greekless reader might well otherwise pronounce the two vowels together. Where the spelling of adjective and adverb differs only in the quantity of the final 'o'—e.g. *kakos* and *kakōs*—I have always marked the long 'o' of the adverb. For greater simplicity, nouns and adjectives are quoted in the nominative, singular or plural, verbs in the infinitive.

Pronunciation need present few difficulties, provided that it is remembered that there are no unpronounced vowels in Greek, i.e. that a word like *psūchē* is disyllabic. Apart from this, there is no agreed pronunciation of Greek among scholars in Britain; for example, different scholars pronounce 'ē' as in 'three', as in 'whey', or (roughly) as in 'bear'. In pronouncing Greek words, the Greekless reader will be well advised to adopt a stress accent, as in pronouncing English, and to place it on whatever syllable his knowledge of Latin or Italian leads him to believe plausible. This accent will be wrong, frequently in position, always in kind, for the Greeks of the classical period employed a pitch accent; but as the resulting pronunciation will bear a close resemblance to that of the majority of classical scholars educated in these islands, including the present writer, the Greekless reader may presumably be forgiven for using it.

Chronological Table[1]

(I have included the dates of birth of many authors. Though frequently conjectural, they are in most cases unlikely to be inaccurate by more than a few years; and it is useful to be reminded of the events which occurred during the early years of an author's life, and of the social and intellectual climate in which he grew up.)

Authors	*Contemporary Events*
800 Homer? about 750	Foundation of Cyme about 750
700 Hesiod *floruit* about 700	
Tyrtaeus *floruit* about 660	
Birth of Solon about 638	
600	Periander Tyrant of Corinth about 625–585
	Solon archon 594
Earliest datable Theognid poem about 580	
Birth of Xenophanes about 576	
	Earliest coinage in Aegina about 570
	Pisistratus Tyrant of Athens for first time about 561–560
	Pisistratus Tyrant of Athens for second time about 559–556
	Croesus ruler of Lydia 560–546
Birth of Simonides about 556	
	Earliest Attic coinage about 550
	Pisistratus Tyrant of Athens for third time 546–528
	Polycrates Tyrant of Samos 540–522
Birth of Aeschylus 525	

[1] For further information I recommend the reader who has not a detailed knowledge of Greek history to consult the Time Charts (1 and 2 are relevant to the period discussed in this book) compiled by Dr. John Moore (Discourses, Ltd., High Street, Tunbridge Wells, Kent).

CHRONOLOGICAL TABLE

Authors	*Contemporary Events*
500 Birth of Sophocles about 496	
Latest datable Theognid poem about 490	Battle of Marathon 490
	Theron Tyrant of Acragas 488–472
Birth of Herodotus about 485	
	Construction of 100 triremes by Athens 483
Birth of Euripides about 480	Battle of Thermopylae 480
Death of Xenophanes about 480	Battle of Salamis 480
Birth of Protagoras about 480	
Birth of Gorgias about 480	
	Battle of Plataea 479
	Confederacy of Delos founded 478–477
	Hiero Tyrant of Syracuse 478–467
Pindar *floruit* about 475–440	
Bacchylides *floruit* about 470–460	
	Birth of Socrates 469
Death of Simonides about 468	
Herodotus *floruit* about 468–425	
Birth of Thucydides about 460	
Birth of Democritus about 460	
Birth of Lysias about 459	
Death of Aeschylus 456	Athenian Land Empire 457–445
	Delian League's treasury moved to Athens 454
Thucydides writing his history, about 432–404	
	Outbreak of Peloponnesian War 431
	Death of Pericles 429
	Cleon 'champion of the people' 429–422
Birth of Plato about 428	Revolt of Mytilene 428
	Destruction of Melos 416
	Sicilian Expedition 415–413

CHRONOLOGICAL TABLE

Authors	*Contemporary Events*
Death of Protagoras about 411	
Death of Euripides 406	
Death of Sophocles 405	
	End of Peloponnesian War 404
	Rule of Thirty at Athens 404–403
400	Trial and death of Socrates 399

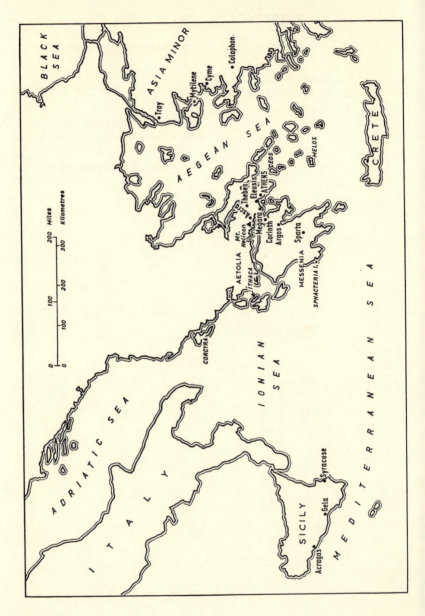

BLACK SEA

ASIA MINOR

• Troy

• Mytilene
• Cyme
• Colophon

AEGEAN SEA

CRETE

• MELOS

KEOS

Thebes
Mt. Helicon
ATHENS
Eleusis
Megara
Corinth
Argos
Sparta

AETOLIA
ITHACA
MESSENIA
SPHACTERIA I.

CORCYRA

IONIAN SEA

ADRIATIC SEA

ITALY

MEDITERRANEAN SEA

SICILY
Syracuse
Gela
Acragas

200 Miles
200
100
100
0
Kilometres
300
200
100
0

ANCIENT CULTURE AND SOCIETY

MORAL VALUES AND POLITICAL
BEHAVIOUR IN ANCIENT GREECE

From Homer to the end of the Fifth Century

I

Problems and Methods

THIS book will discuss moral values and political behaviour in the period between Homer and the end of the fifth century.[1] Its scope requires some explanation: in the context of ancient Greece, 'politics' may well suggest a discussion of the fifth and fourth centuries rather than a treatment which, however briefly, includes the Homeric poems and omits the fourth century altogether.[2] My purpose is not to suggest that study of fourth-century values and political behaviour is less valuable: the fourth century is no less interesting and illuminating than the fifth. But the volumes in this series are limited in size; and I do wish to suggest, and in the following chapters to argue, that the developed political values and behaviour of fifth- and fourth-century Greece can only be adequately understood in the light of the situations and evaluations that preceded them; for values and presuppositions that were well suited to the communities of early Greece persisted even in later periods where their presence is at first sight very surprising. Accordingly, faced with the choice of omitting either the early formative period or the fourth century, I have chosen to omit the latter; and in the space at my disposal I have endeavoured to trace the gradual development of 'politics' within the framework of Homeric and early Greek values and presuppositions, indicating as I did so the aspects of society which, even in later periods, encouraged the persistence of features which were at variance with many of the apparent aims of its institutions.

[1] All dates are B.C. unless otherwise indicated.

[2] The forensic speeches discussed are of necessity drawn from the earlier years of the fourth century, there being no earlier material; and some material is drawn from Plato; but I have used Plato only as evidence for the accepted values of society which Socrates and Plato were challenging. In each case I regard the evidence as being characteristic of both the late fifth and early fourth centuries.

Some may regard the second chapter in particular as having little relation to politics as they understand the term; but if such readers will persevere through the remainder of the book, the relevance of the early discussions will, I believe, become apparent.

The study of values and political behaviour in any society requires a number of tools and techniques. These may be quite readily acquired, and are not difficult to handle; but they are necessary: the study cannot be conducted by the light of nature. In this chapter I shall discuss the tools and techniques that are used in the rest of the book.

I must first explain how I propose to use 'values' and 'society'. 'Society', as I use it here, is a term which makes the minimum of assumptions: it is used to denote any assemblage of persons which it is convenient or customary to treat as one assemblage; for example, the inhabitants of Homeric Ithaca, the Greek army besieging Troy, the Athenians of the fifth century. By using 'society' of any of these assemblages, I do not prejudge the issue of the kind of relationships which individuals, or groups, in these assemblages had with each other: only careful observation will reveal this. By 'values' I mean what is expressed and revealed by the explicit value-judgments of members of the society, which they use to evaluate an individual or a group ('he is a good man') and the actions of either ('he/they behaved well'), or when taking decisions ('it is right for you/us to do this'), when those judgments are considered in the light of the characteristics which are held to justify passing them. 'Values' in this sense should be sharply distinguished from hopes and aspirations, and may violently conflict with them: it is possible, and indeed not uncommon, for a society to aspire to peace abroad and harmony at home while holding values which lead its members to be frequently at variance with each other and with other societies.

To study 'values' in this sense in any society, we must have access to a large number of value-judgments passed by its members in particular contexts of words and events. Material can be collected, evidently, in either literate or non-literate societies of the present day; but collection is also possible in

literate societies of the past, provided that the surviving documents are sufficiently numerous. It is, of course, at times
irritating not to be able to ask questions of human agents
long dead; but against this must be set the fact that the self-
conscious answer to a question about values or behaviour is
frequently untypical and misleading, and that—certainly in
the case of the ancient Greeks whom we are to study here—
those who left the records could have had no inkling of what
our standards, over two millennia later, were likely to be, and
so could make no effort, even had they wished to do so, to
please or impress us by affecting adherence to values which
were in fact not theirs: a hazard ever present to the sociologist
and field anthropologist, though one which, with care, can
certainly be circumvented.

A body of primary material is necessary; but must it be
studied in the original language, or will translated documents
suffice? The question has relevance to any society, but not
least to that of ancient Greece, interest in which seems to be
increasing even more rapidly than the number of those who
can read the language diminishes. A glance at the subsequent
chapters of this book will reveal my own view: the documents
there discussed are in large part translated, but some words—
not many, but words that occur repeatedly—are not translated but transliterated. These words are the more important
value-terms of the ancient Greeks; and they are untranslatable:
not fortuitously untranslatable, but importantly and systematically untranslatable for reasons linked with the nature
of the society in which they occur. If we are to understand
either the values or the society, we must not attempt to study
these words in translation.

To make such assertions is, I am aware, immediately to
arouse disbelief: after all, are we not forever consulting lexica
and dictionaries to discover 'the meaning' in the context before us of a foreign word which we do not know? And is not
'the meaning' what there is in common between the foreign
language and our own, while the words belong to different
languages? That is, indeed, the implicit and unanalysed presupposition that all too frequently governs our behaviour when
we are reading, or attempting to read, a foreign language; and

3

it is a presupposition which prevents many who 'know Greek' in the sense of being able to supply English 'equivalents' for many Greek words from ever 'thinking in Greek', whether they are concerned with value-terms or with other words. The problem of communication with which I am concerned here is not confined to those who are completely ignorant of the language of the society that they are attempting to study.

It is, I suspect, the fact that 'meaning' is a noun that causes much of the difficulty: the 'meaning' is readily manufactured into an entity, an entity more real than the word; and when, in translating from a foreign language, we are, as frequently happens, faced with a word with 'more than one meaning', we select, from the range of 'meanings' which we, or the lexica, know to be sometimes appropriate, the 'meaning' which best suits the context before us, rather as one might, faced with a pincushion containing a number of labelled pins, select the pin and label that seemed appropriate, without troubling oneself why the pincushion should contain precisely these pins and no others. But what are the 'meanings', the labelled pins? And why do we suppose them to be present? Are not the 'meanings' frequently no more than the different words by which, when called upon to translate it, we are compelled on different occasions to render this one foreign word? If so, their 'existence' is a result of the behaviour of modern English; and in treating them as real entities, and using now one, now another, English word to render the same Greek word, we are, if we regard our translations as satisfactory, implying that the ancient Greeks knew modern English, and imposing a modern English pattern on their thought and literature. A less misleading and hampering model—though all models and analogies must be treated with care—is to regard the word as a tool with uses: a tool is evidently more real than are the occasions and modes of its use, and the word is then 'seen' as an entity which persists through its uses; and we may then be led to enquire the reason for this range of usage, and the characteristics that the word derives from it; whereupon we are beginning to 'think in Greek', or any other language that we treat in this manner.

4

The position needs careful statement. There is a fairly obvious sense in which one word may have two clearly separable 'meanings' for its users. When he asked for a *testudo*, the Roman general did not expect to be supplied with a tortoise; and few Greeks can have attempted to open doors with a collar-bone. Yet even here, where distinct physical objects are denoted by the same word, the use of the same word must have affected the manner in which the Greeks 'saw' keys and collar-bones, the Roman, tortoises and siege-shelters.[1] It is not, of course, of such words as these that I am thinking in saying that translation is systematically and importantly misleading. In most contexts what is lost in rendering *testudo* and *kleis* by 'tortoise' or 'siege-shelter', 'key' or 'collar-bone', in accordance with what is 'meant' in that context, will be quite unimportant. Yet my readers will readily be able to construct for themselves untranslatable jokes using *testudo* or *kleis*; and a Roman or Greek poet could, if it suited his purpose, make use of the range of these words in a manner unavailable to an English poet, and untranslatable into English.

If he did, of course, the English reader would notice, for the result would be a pun, serious or comic; but where the word concerned is not a noun denoting a physical object, we frequently do not notice, but merely choose 'the meaning' from the range of 'meanings' which we, or the lexicographers, know to be available. Now this book will be devoted to the study of Greek value-terms in ethical, political and religious contexts: words which do not denote physical objects to which we might point 'to make the meaning clear'. The situation is now very different. Even if all knowledge of Latin and Greek were lost, there are other, non-linguistic, means whereby we might discover that the Romans possessed tortoises and siege-shelters,

---

[1] Metaphors can, of course, die. The extent to which any metaphor is still alive is a matter for judgment in the particular case. For example, 'lid' in 'eyelid' (first attested about 1240) might appear to be quite dead and is dead for most purposes; but when the witch in Shakespeare's *Macbeth* (1, 3, 19 f.) says 'Sleep shall never, night or day, Hang upon his penthouse lid' (i.e. eyelid), it is 'lid' in 'eyelid' that makes the play on words comprehensible, and may reactivate 'lid' in 'eyelid' for the reader subsequently.

the Greeks, keys and collar-bones; and we may well feel that we should have lost very little that is valuable if we were unaware of the words which the Romans and Greeks used for these articles. But if, all ancient Greek having perished, we did not know, for example, the Greek word *aretē*, its rôle in Greek society and its range of application, we could not reconstruct the Greek concept of *arete* by other means; for this can be discovered only by observing the behaviour of the term in specific contexts. Even though we have the word and its contexts, however, we may yet conceal from ourselves the nature of the concept of *arete*: if we can read the texts only in translation, or if while 'knowing Greek' we think of *arete* as having different 'meanings' in different contexts, and so think in English rather than in Greek, we shall falsify the phenomena; for if we are to understand the Greek concept of *arete* we must study the nature of the situations in which it is applied. Since *arete* 'has the meanings' 'goodness', 'bravery', 'success', 'prosperity' [in the sense that these—and others—are the English words which, in translation, we shall on different occasions be constrained to use to render *arete*] and there is no one English word which is always applicable, it follows that it is better to transliterate the key terms in order that the reader may discern when, and how, the Greeks used them; for it is an important fact in the study of Greek society that the Greeks used the one word *arete* where we use different words. (The usage of the transliterated terms will be discussed throughout: the Greekless reader is in no danger of being left with unexplained Greek words in front of him.)

Having decided to transliterate, however, we must still consider the special problems of understanding value-terms in a foreign language. For value-terms have both a 'descriptive meaning' and an 'evaluative meaning':[1] we must discover both the characteristics to which they are applied and the manner in which they commend or decry the possession of those characteristics. In establishing the 'descriptive meaning' we are faced with the difficulty that a general value-term like 'good' has a wider range of applicability than most other

[1] For the terms see R. M. Hare, *The Language of Morals*, Oxford 1952, pp. 118 ff.

6

words. However, in this study we are concerned only with the characteristics of good (or *agathoi*) men and women, not with those of good apples or good big inkstands; and the scale of the survey is thereby reduced. When we have discovered the range of *arete* as applied to a man in Homer, we may say 'Homeric society's concept of human male *arete* has the characteristics *a*, *b*, *c* . . . *n*'. Having reached this point, however, we have not completed the task: to understand the behaviour and relationship of the terms in a value-system, more is relevant than the range of usage of the value-terms employed; and this 'more' is precisely the value-aspect of value-words, their emotive power, their evaluative meaning. In the case of descriptive meaning, range of usage must be determined; in the case of evaluative meaning, the intensity of the commendation or disapproval expressed, which is different for different value-terms in the usage of any individual or group. Consider the phrase 'unsuccessful but honest'. Given the characteristic phrase-balance of English, anyone who utters the phrase in this form evidently values honesty more highly than success. It is, however, perfectly comprehensible to say 'honest but unsuccessful', implying that one values success more highly than honesty; and one could certainly find individuals and groups in our society willing to make the second evaluation.

This example is intended to demonstrate the existence of graduated scales of value-terms, differing in emotive power, to commend different qualities, and the fact that different value-terms and different qualities may appear at different points on the value-scales of different individuals, groups and societies. It should also indicate one aspect of the relationship between values and the characteristics of social groups—the subject of this work; for any group for which 'he was unsuccessful but honest' conveys, on balance, approval, will differ from a group for which 'he was honest but unsuccessful' conveys, on balance, disapproval in many more respects than this one judgment. Now in another society, particularly a society far removed in space and time from our own, not only may the range of application of its value-terms be different from ours, so that there are no real equivalents in this sense, but even approximate equivalents may be valued very differently in the

7

two value-systems. In the case of value-terms, then, there are two factors to render translation, and comprehension, difficult.

For the kind of study proposed in the present work, a broad classification of value-terms and of human excellences and activities is necessary. 'Neutral' terms are needed, terms which do not carry with them our own ethical assumptions, as the word 'moral' itself does; and the study itself requires a broad distinction between two groups of activities and excellences. In any society there are activities in which success and failure are the most important criteria of evaluating what is done; and here commendation or the reverse is reserved for those who actually succeed or fail. Unless we are being consciously epigrammatic, we do not say 'X is a good general but he never wins battles' or 'Y is a good tennis-player but he always loses'. (It should be noted that in some circumstances co-operation among the members of one side, for example an army, or observance of certain rules by both sides, as in tennis, may also be required; but mere knowledge of, and obedience to, the rules does not render one a good tennis-player, and loyalty to one's troops does not by itself render one a good general. Success is the demand, even in our own society; and it should not be assumed that in another society loyalty and rule-observance have even as much status as they have here. Such matters can be settled only by observations of actual judgments of behaviour.) On the other hand, in any society there are also those activities, such as contracts or partnerships, in which men co-operate for a common end. Since the only basis for co-operation is justice and fairness (however these may be understood in the society in question; and this too is a question which can be answered only by careful observation) it is in terms of justice, or some similar word, that the relationships of men who co-operate will be evaluated; and where such criteria are used, it is to be expected that intentions will be taken into account.[1] These two groups of activities differ importantly from each other; and some convenient means of distinguishing them is needed. In this

[1] However, see p. 17; and my ' "Friendship" and "Self-Sufficiency" in Homer and Aristotle', *Classical Quarterly* n.s. xiii (1963) pp. 30 ff. Competitive excellences may be held to be more important

discussion they will be distinguished as competitive and co-operative excellences. The extent to which, in Greek, there are separate groups of competitive and co-operative value-terms to correspond with these excellences will become clear as the discussion proceeds. (The terms 'co-operative excellences' and 'competitive excellences' are, I acknowledge, not ideal; but I can suggest nothing better, without adopting entirely formal labels, such as p-excellences and q-excellences. I have avoided this in the interest of readability.)

We may now say that a group or society which expresses the judgment 'unsuccessful but honest' to convey, on balance, approval, differs from one which expresses the judgment 'honest but unsuccessful' to convey, on balance, disapproval in that the first appears to value co-operative, the second competitive, excellences more highly; though one would not of course base this conclusion on one observation. The two groups, as I have already said, will differ from one another in many other respects than this; and this is one aspect of the link between a society's values and its other characteristics. It is not, however, the only aspect: the other characteristics that a society possesses may powerfully influence its values. We need set up no crude 'chicken and egg' problem: societies develop through time, and values both help to mould, and are moulded by, the society in which they are found. I shall not discuss this question at length here: it is now time to turn from the general to the particular.[1]

---

by other societies where we should hold justice to be relevant, as in the case of homicide in Homer; for which see my *Merit and Responsibility*, Oxford 1960, pp. 52 ff.

[1] In subsequent chapters English words frequently appear in parentheses after transliterated Greek words. These are, of course, not adequate translations, merely hints to the Greekless reader of the general area of usage of the Greek words concerned. The discussion will make explicit the actual usage of each. The Index (pp. 155 ff.) lists the most important occasions on which each Greek word occurs.

The World of the Homeric Poems

I have no space in this work to present more than an outline account of the values of the Homeric poems; and I suspect that most readers who take up a work on values and politics in ancient Greece are unlikely to be seeking primarily information about Homeric society. Nevertheless, something must be said of Homeric society; for the values which we find there persisted into other, later periods. (The important rôle played by the Homeric poems in the education of Greek boys in later Greece furnishes some part of the explanation for this; but, as will appear, it is by no means the complete explanation.) The brief account that I give here of Homeric values and society will, I hope, render the later phenomena more comprehensible. The account will be necessarily dogmatic; for justification of the sweeping statements that appear in this chapter, I refer my readers to what I have written elsewhere.[1]

First, Homeric society is the society depicted in the Homeric poems. It is very possible, indeed likely, that no *event* portrayed in those poems ever took place: in that sense, the poems are unhistorical. To say this, however, does not entail that the society and values are unconnected with any society that existed in early Greece: there is a degree of coherence and consistency in the values themselves, and an appropriateness to the society, that seems beyond the inventive ability—or indeed the likely inventive desire—of an oral bardic tradition. It seems difficult not to conclude that the values and society depicted are related to some actually existing society, whose identity it is unnecessary to discuss here. In any case, the society and its values were held to be real by later Greeks, and

[1] See *Merit and Responsibility: a study in Greek values*, Oxford 1960, chapters ii and iii; and the articles listed in the Bibliography, p. 151 below.

there are discernible links with the values and organization of later Greece. Homeric society has been elegantly and convincingly analysed in social anthropological terms by M. I. Finley in *The World of Odysseus*;[1] and this analysis furnishes the 'facts of Homeric life' whose relationship to Homeric values will be considered here.

Both the *Iliad* (as in I, 277 ff. IX, 37 ff.) and the *Odyssey* (as in I, 391 ff.) speak of kingship over larger groups than the individual household; and *Iliad* IX, 149 ff. depicts Agamemnon as able to offer Achilles rule over seven cities, presumably only a small proportion of the total deemed to be under his own control.[2] Here, however, we must concern ourselves with the actual practice and working assumptions of the characters in the poems; and in practice Homeric man lived in a society of virtually autonomous small social units called *oikoi*, noble households each under the headship of a local chieftain, denoted and commended by the term *agathos*. The *oikos* was at once the largest effective social, political and economic unit. There was a tenuous structure of relationships between *oikoi*, in that an assembly could be held, if need arose, to determine questions which seemed to demand action from the members of more than one *oikos*; but according to Homer no assembly was held in Ithaca between the departure of Odysseus and the occasion, some twenty years later, when his son Telemachus summoned one in *Odyssey* II. The reason was not that only Telemachus, and he only when adult, could summon such an assembly in the absence of Odysseus; II, 28 f. makes it clear that many individuals had the right to summon it. That

[1] London, Chatto and Windus, 1956.

[2] The poems in other respects show discrepancies between what is stated to be the case 'in theory' and the actual practice which the bards can understand and portray. The *Catalogue* of *Iliad* II lists a Greek army of over 100,000 men; but the presuppositions and practice of the actual fighting of the poems are those of the very much smaller units which the bards could comprehend. Similarly, the tradition had transmitted the isolated idea of Agamemnon as a ruler over many cities; but Agamemnon's actual situation in practice in the poems is portrayed in terms of a much vaguer and looser social organisation.

assembly, when called, achieved nothing; and its proceedings as narrated give little expectation that it would achieve much. The troubles of Ithaca are nowhere stated to be the result of a lack of assemblies; the troubles of Odysseus' *oikos* are frequently stated to be the result of the absence of Odysseus. In general, the head of an *oikos* could rely on no-one else for support; and since the other members of the *oikos* needed him to secure their very existence, the demand that he should succeed was categoric.

The most powerful words to commend an individual in Homeric Greek are the adjectives *agathos* and *esthlos*, with the abstract noun *arete*; the most powerful words to decry him being *kakos* and *deilos*, with the abstract noun *kakotēs*. The most powerful word to decry his actions is the neuter adjective *aischron*; and the abstract noun *elencheiē* denotes and decries the condition of an *agathos* who has behaved like a *kakos* and done something *aischron*, or—since Homeric society is a 'shame-culture'[1]—is conscious that his fellows believe him to have acted in this manner. I have explained in the first chapter why it is inadvisable to render these words by words such as 'good' and 'bad' without first examining the manner in which they behave in Homeric society; and so soon as we make such an examination, all desire to render them in this manner should disappear. *Agathos* and *esthlos* in Homer denote and commend men who are effective and successful fighters, whether formally at war or defending their *oikos* in what passes for peace in such a society. The words also commend men who are prosperous and of high birth. There is no question of separate 'meanings'. *Agathos* and *esthlos* denote and commend all these qualities together because the needs of the *oikos* demand that all are united in certain individuals. The group —*oikos* in peace, contingent following its local *agathos* in war—

---

[1] A shame-culture is one whose sanction is overtly 'what people will say'. See *Merit and Responsibility* pp. 48 f. Homeric man lives in such a culture. It is also, and more fundamentally, a 'results-culture'; for which see my *From the Many to the One*, Constable and Cornell University Press 1970, pp. 29 ff., 42 ff., and 'Threatening, Abusing and Feeling Angry in the Homeric Poems', *Journal of Hellenic Studies* LXXXIX (1969), pp. 7 ff.

needs for its continued survival to be defended as efficiently as possible. Efficient defence requires the best available armour and weapons. These must be supplied by the individual himself, so that the most effectively armed individual must be wealthy. The Homeric poems portray a moneyless economy, in which wealth consists of land and its products, houses, goods and chattels. The land is in the hands of a restricted number of large landowners, and passes by inheritance. Those who are able effectively to defend the group, accordingly, must unite in themselves courage, strength, wealth and high birth; and since these are the qualities of which society holds itself to be most in need, they are denoted and commended by *agathos*, *esthlos* and *arete*.

Furthermore, since it is by success, not by good intentions, that the group continues to exist, good intentions do not suffice: it is *aischron* to fail, whatever one's intentions, in those activities which are held to contribute to the defence of the *oikos*, or of the group for whose success one is held responsible in war. It is misleading, accordingly, even to say that courage is highly valued; it is only courage-leading-to-success that is so regarded: failure is *aischron*, whether one exerted oneself bravely or ran like a rabbit. (The *agathos* is, of course, expected to strive to the utmost; and if he is rebuked when the battle is still in progress he may reply that he is doing so, as in *Iliad* XIII, 222 ff.; but once the battle is lost, it is useless to point out that one did one's best. Doubtless we have similar values in war; but the same demands are made of the Homeric *agathos* in war and peace alike.)

These are the activities that are most highly valued, since the members of the society see most need for them. The poems are written from the point of view of the *agathos*; and if we insist that Homeric society is the society depicted in the poems, *kakoi* hardly 'exist' for us at all, since they are rarely mentioned. However, we have in Thersites (*Iliad* II, 212 ff.) not merely a *kakos* but what the *agathoi* regard as a radical and recalcitrant *kakos*; and his claim is not that he, Thersites, is as *agathos* as Agamemnon, but that Achilles, whom Agamemnon has slighted, is more *agathos* than Agamemnon (II, 239 f.). As depicted, then, the *kakoi* agree with the *agathoi* about the

evaluations of Homeric society. We may say that the documents, like all our documents from ancient Greece, are biased
in favour of the *agathos*; but there are powerful reasons to
explain the high value accorded to the *agathoi*, the low value
accorded to the *kakoi*; and it will become apparent in later
periods, where the relationship of literature to a particular
society is more demonstrable, that the *kakos* is likely to defer
to the *agathos*. In saying that 'the members of society' see most
need for these values, then, we may reasonably infer that *all*
members of the society were likely to discern the need.

These—competitive—activities and excellences being most
highly valued, other—co-operative—activities and excellences
were less esteemed; and they are indeed not part of the *arete*
of the *agathos*: an *agathos* might behave as Agamemnon behaves
to Achilles, or the suitors to Odysseus, without smirching his
arete. To say this is not to say that co-operative excellences were
not valued at all, nor that when an individual was wrongfully
harmed he did not set a high value on having his wrong
avenged and recompensed: it is to say that when an *agathos*
wronged someone else, an observer, not himself harmed, more
readily saw the need of the group for the *arete* of the *agathos*,
and the benefit conferred by that *arete*, than that any comparable harm was being done to the group by this individual
breach of co-operative excellences. The view should not be
equated with 'might is right', for this judgment is usually
expressed disapprovingly: we should say rather 'the qualities
which the society believes itself to need most, and so values
most highly, take precedence in the evaluation of a person or
one of his actions over qualities which the society believes
itself to need less'.

Closely linked with this are the Homeric concepts of *tīmē*,
conventionally rendered 'honour, compensation, penalty';
tiein and *tīmān*, 'to honour'; (*apo*) *tīnein*, 'to pay a price, be
punished'; (*apo*) *tīnesthai*, 'to punish'. Examination of the
range of these terms reveals that *time* denotes the possessions
of which the *agathos* has more than any other human being,
while at the other end of the scale is 'the wanderer without
time' (*Iliad* IX, 648) who has no position and no possessions,
nowhere to lay his head save by favour of others, and no means

of securing his own continued existence. He may be harmed with impunity, as Achilles states in the passage mentioned. No such commodity with such a function could merely record in arithmetical terms units of property. *Time* carries a very high emotive charge, and it is not surprising that to defend one's own *time*, if possible to acquire more, and at all events not to lose any of what one has, is the principal motivation of Homeric man; with the result that transactions which appear very different to us appear the same to him. To punish is 'to get back *time* for oneself', since in Homer the *agathos* was in such matters thrown back upon his own resources; but when Alcinous (*Odyssey* XIII, 14 f.), having promised more presents to Odysseus than he has already received, and having suggested that each of the Phaeacian counsellors should give him a tripod and cauldron, says 'we will make a collection among the people and *tinesthai*; for it is hard that one man should give presents and get no return for it', evidently no-one would render this by 'punish' in English. It is not 'punish'; but it is *tinesthai*, for just as Homeric man in punishing 'gets back *time* for himself',[1] as did the Greeks, for example, when they sacked Troy, or Orestes when he killed Aegisthus and recovered his kingdom and all its *time* (*Odyssey* III, 195 ff.), so here Alcinous and the Phaeacian counsellors will, by collecting valuable objects from other Phaeacians, increase their own *time*, depleted by giving valuable gifts—*time*—to Odysseus. Since *time* is so important, a basic essential of Homeric existence, these transactions, which appear different to us, appear in the same light to Homeric society. Punishment, in fact, as we know it, does not exist in Homeric society: it is assimilated to other modes of behaviour, which, as a result, do not themselves exist as we know them. In the case of *time* too, results— the actual presence or absence of *time*—are much more important than intentions.

The *agathos* must defend his *time*, and he is well-armed to do it; but of course no man can rely for his security entirely on his own strong right arm, however fine his armour. On what can

---

[1] *Tinesthai* and *time* are derived from different roots; but Homeric usage closely associates them, and it is usage, not etymology, that 'gives a word its meaning'.

the Homeric *agathos* rely? Apart from his own limbs and psychological functions—the distinction here being ours rather than Homer's[1]—he has his tools, weapons, possessions and portion of land; and he has his wife, children, servants and other dependants. On these he can rely, or should be able to, for the animate members of this group depend on him for their defence, and for their share of the *time* of the *oikos* which he defends and of which they partake in the form of their food, clothing, shelter and status; and they should in return behave in the manner he expects of them. But apart from these members of the *oikos*, he can depend only on those persons with whom he has entered into formal relations of 'guest-friendship', denoted by *philotēs* or *xeniē*.[2] The behaviour of *time* shows that human beings have no rights *qua* human beings in Homer. They have only what, if *agathoi*, they can defend for themselves; if not *agathoi*, what they are guaranteed by some more powerful individual, to whom they are related either by birth, by direct economic dependence, by marriage, or from some other cause. The rest of the world is indifferent or hostile: it competes, or ignores.

It is not surprising that Homeric man should use some word to demarcate the persons and things on which his existence depends, and distinguish them from persons and things in general. The word is *philos*, conventionally rendered 'own' or 'dear'; in fact untranslatable, for we are not acutely aware of possessing a limited stock of persons and things upon whom our very existence depends. The Homeric *agathos* is; and the awareness furnishes *philos* with a range and a high emotive charge which correspond to that of no English word. It denotes and commends the good things, *agatha*, which he possesses and can use to secure his continued existence; and since the idea that human beings should be treated as ends-in-themselves rather than as means is not Greek, there is no reason why persons and things should be thought of differently. All are *philon*, and all are *philon* in the same way.

[1] See *From the Many to the One*, pp. 13 ff.
[2] See Finley, op. cit., pp. 109 ff., and my ' "Friendship" and "Self-sufficiency" in Homer and Aristotle', *Classical Quarterly* n.s. xiii (1963), 33 ff.

To render other human beings his *philoi*, the *agathos* must of course benefit them; and this activity is *philein*, a word conventionally rendered 'like', 'love', 'receive hospitably'. *Philein* requires action and results rather than emotions or intentions: a familiar situation in Homeric society. True, the essence of the *philotes*-relationship is co-operation, not competition, so that on the basis of what was said in the first chapter we might expect intentions to be relevant;[1] but *philotes* is co-operation to meet the harsh demands of Homeric life. Take the case of the man who is away from his own *oikos*. He has, as has been said, no rights *qua* human being, merely those he is guaranteed by some member of the new society into which he has come. He is a *hiketēs*, a comer (or suppliant, for all 'comers' must be suppliants); and once he addresses himself to the head of a household, he is believed to have 'the suppliants' Zeus' as his champion. If accepted, he may be given the status of *philos* or *xeinos* by some one sufficiently powerful member of society, some *agathos*, some head of *oikos*. If he is given such status, this new relationship, *philotes*, subsists only between the comer and the man who *philein* him. The unit of power, the social unit, the economic unit is the *oikos*: no effective larger unit than the *oikos* exists to protect the comer, no unit larger than the *oikos* possesses any property, and hence no larger unit could provide the comer with nourishment. Accordingly, the comer has no relationship of *philotes* with the remainder of the society into which he has come, the collection of *oikoi*. Accordingly, when he is in the land of the *agathos* who *philein* him, he is dependent on the *actions* of that man for his continued existence, outnumbered as he is in a land of actual or potential enemies with no strong centralised government and no belief that human beings have certain basic rights *qua* human beings. Furthermore, the comer, particularly if he comes by land, can carry little with him: this is a society with no coined money, no readily transportable wealth. What he needs is not primarily sympathy and affection, which are luxuries for a man in his position, but actions: the provision of food, shelter and protection if he needs it; in short, *time*.

In these circumstances, it is *philotes* that denotes that part of

[1] Above, p. 8.

the world whose behaviour is, or should be, reliable; and this common characteristic is singled out in relationships whose differences we should rather emphasise. Every relationship from sexual passion to guest-friendship is denoted by *philotes*. The reason is evidently not that the Greeks were unusually warm friends or unusually cold lovers, but that a different aspect of these relationships is denoted by *philotes*. Again, these relationships have a very objective character. Once they have been established, their existence does not depend on the inclinations of those who are involved in them. Amphiaraus remains Eriphyle's '*philos* man' even when she is betraying him to his death (*Odyssey* XI, 326 f.); and when the Greek Diomedes (*Iliad* VI, 119 ff.) meets the Trojan Glaucus, he declares, on discovering his identity, that Glaucus is his *xeinos* in virtue of a compact of guest-friendship made between their grandfathers. In consequence, he will not fight with him even in the Trojan War, in which they find themselves on opposing sides. This is not a conflict between nation-states; and *philotes* is the basic structure of co-operative life: Diomedes is far more closely bound to a Lycian who is his *philos* than to a Greek who is not, even during the Trojan War. *Philotes* furnishes Homeric life with such stability as it possesses, and is a permanent bond which cannot be overset by a transient occurrence such as the Trojan War; and it does not depend on the feelings or inclinations of those who inherit it, since Glaucus and Diomedes have never seen one another before.

Homeric *arete*, *time* and *philotes* suit the *oikos*-based society. There must, of course, be other values, co-operative ones; but these are less highly valued by the society, for reasons already given. One word used in competitive and co-operative situations alike is *aidōs*, which expresses the distaste felt at doing something of which the society disapproves, or failing to do something of which society approves; and it is discernible that the *aidos* felt at breaches of co-operative excellences is weaker. 'Naturally to say that this distaste, this *aidos*, is weaker when the quiet virtues are in question is not to say that it does not exist; and it must be such *aidos* which holds Homeric society together, in so far as it is held together, for a society of *agathoi*

18

with no quiet virtues at all would simply destroy itself. But . . . as soon as a crisis forces the essential framework of values into view, the competitive values are so much more powerful than the co-operative that the situation is not considered in terms of the quiet values at all.'[1]

Behaviour 'in accordance with *moira*' or 'not in accordance with *moira*' will serve as an example of the weaker type of restraint found in Homeric life. One's *moira* is one's share, one's due share—of food at a banquet, of inheritance, in general of the real goods which constitute wealth in Homeric society: one's *moira* of *time*, in fact. Since Homer does not think abstractly, one's *moira* is one's status in society; and in a stratified society, to speak or behave 'in accordance with one's share' is to speak or behave 'as is right', to speak or behave 'not in accordance with one's share' is to speak or behave 'as is wrong'. 'As is right' or 'as is wrong' are the usual renderings for these phrases in English; but in such a society it will be the *agathoi* who determine what is or is not 'according to one's share'. For the *kakos* to yield to the *agathos*, as the people in effect yield to the suitors in *Odyssey* II, is to act 'according to his share'; and the *kakos* will yield. For an *agathos* to yield to an *agathos* with superior strength or with a god on his side would be to act 'according to his share'; but here (as in *Iliad* VIII, 146 ff.) *arete* demands that one should fight. In both cases, the claims of *arete* prevail.

The values of the Homeric gods are similar. They 'have more *arete*, *time* and strength than men' (*Iliad* IX, 498); and this, save that they do not die, is the only significant difference between Homeric god and Homeric man of which Homer tells us. They demand *time* from men in the form of sacrifices, offerings and temples;[2] and it is results, not intentions, that are taken into account: to forget a sacrifice is as heinous as deliberately to refuse one. If sacrifice is offered, a *philotes*-relationship is set up between man and god; and the man has a claim for divine help. Whether the worshipper has acted

[1] *Merit and Responsibility* p. 46.

[2] Temples are rarely mentioned, and at this period must have been very simple structures; but Chryses mentions 'roofing a temple' as one of his benefactions to Apollo (*Iliad* I, 39).

unjustly to his fellow-men or no is *for the most part* not taken into account: in *Odyssey* I, 60 ff., Athena points out that Odysseus gave sacrifice when before Troy; so why should Zeus be angry with him? (That he is angry, or that some deity is, is an empirical issue: since the Homeric Hades is dank and unpleasant for all, any divine help (or hindrance) must be given in this life, for there is no hope of recompense later; and success and disaster are god-given; so to suffer woes is to be hated by the gods.) Another bond of *philotes* is actual kinship with a deity: several of the 'heroes' on both the Greek and the Trojan side had one divine parent, and many had a divine ancestor. In these cases, as is shown by the evaluation of Hector and Achilles (*Iliad* XXIV, 55 ff.), the *philotes* that divine parentage confers is of a higher grade, and entitles one to more *time*, than even the most *philos* who is a mere human (66) can attain by having offered abundant sacrifice. Here too appropriate treatment is understood in terms of the *arete*, *time* and *philotes* of those concerned.

The gods—Zeus, where a god is named—are believed to punish certain breaches of co-operative relationships: notably towards beggars, wanderers, suppliants and guests. These stand in special need of protection; for while it would be *aischron* for an *agathos* not to protect his suppliants and guests against others, it would not be *aischron* for him to harm them himself. The function may appear strange for the Olympians we have seen so far, who are concerned only with their *time* and *philotes*-relationships; but if Zeus Xeinios were thought of as taking beggars, wanderers, suppliants and guests under his protection as a human *agathos* might, then it would be a blot on his *arete* not to harm anyone who harmed one whom he had taken under his protection, and so the behaviour would conform to *arete*-standards. Other passages where *dikaios*, 'just', is used may in fact have a limited range: Odysseus on coming to a new country several times (*Odyssey* VI, 120, VIII, 575, IX, 175) enquires whether the inhabitants are *dikaioi* and godfearing; which implies that to be 'just' is to be godfearing. He couples *dikaioi* with *philoxeinoi*, 'given to *philein* strangers'; and the sphere of *dikaios* may well here be restricted to behaviour towards wanderers, beggars, guests and suppliants.

THE WORLD OF THE HOMERIC POEMS

There are signs of a wider development in Homer;[1] but these are tentative, and discussion of more moral deities may be left until the next chapter.

This brief and dogmatic account of Homeric values will serve, I hope, to indicate that Homeric values suit the society of the poems. Any *agathos* holding such values is always in potential competition with other *agathoi*, and the main plots of both poems, the conflicts between Agamemnon and Achilles, Odysseus and the suitors, show what happens when such competition becomes actual. Those holding such values require considerable space in which to manœuvre; but the poems give the impression that, in Homer, the space is available, and that *agathoi* could coexist peacefully for the most part each within his *moira* of *time*. No set of *agathoi* could be in constant active competition, as I have already said; but the most powerful values of the society commend success and decry failure in securing the prosperity and stability of one's group, *oikos*; and so soon as the *agathos* feels threatened, feels that he may lose *time*, then all the demands of the *arete*-group of values are actualised: he must ensure the success of his *oikos*, and prevent it, and himself, from losing ground in comparison with other *oikoi*, or *agathoi*, by any effective means, just or no. If any means are disapproved of by the gods, they will show their disapproval by reducing his *time*, bringing disaster upon him; so that such means are not in fact effective. The Homeric gods' disapproval of injustice is occasional and usually confined to breaches of certain definite relationships, notably those with suppliants, strangers and beggars. They take little note of acts of injustice in general, and favour individuals for reasons quite unconnected with their just behaviour. Unless he enjoys such favour, the *agathos* must defend himself, and his own, without the help of heaven.

[1] See *Merit and Responsibility*, p. 66.

3

From Hesiod to the Sixth Century

A. INTRODUCTORY

THE Homeric world has a coherence of its own. Its values, its social, economic and political structure, its view of life, form a whole. On turning to the authors to be discussed in this chapter, we move into a new world, a world that seems in some ways, surprising as it may appear, more hazardous than that of the Homeric heroes. It is true that the Homeric *agathos* had to defend his *moira* of *time*, his possessions and position, by means of his own *arete*; and that failure would have meant loss of that *moira* of *time*, as situations in the Homeric poems make clear. Yet the total range of usage of *moira* in Homer links one's possession of one's property and status, high or low, with what is most stable in the experience of Homeric man, as the frequent (mis-)translation of *moira* by 'Fate' in part of its range of usage serves to indicate.[1] Individual *agathoi* might fail; all *agathoi* must have been under great strain; but the *agathoi* as a class, the wealthy possessors of land, continued to exist, and doubtless most of these families continued in possession of their land, while the landless *kakos* had no opportunity of obtaining any: where land was the standard of wealth, he could not purchase it (even had anyone been able and willing to sell; and land was presumably inalienable) for there was nothing else with which he could purchase it; and being, as a *kakos*, necessarily ill-armed, he had no chance of taking land by force. Again, the land of a community—and so, in

---

[1] *Moira* is never used to express a belief in total determinism. No such belief is found in Greece during the period discussed in this work (see also pp. 88 ff. below). The translation 'Fate' is accordingly inappropriate; but *moira* does set limits to the behaviour of god and man, and denotes what is most stable in the experience of Homeric Society. (See *Merit and Responsibility* pp. 17 ff.)

such a society, its wealth—is evidently limited in size, the more so in the small communities of Greece: the Homeric Greek lived in a finite and bounded world, with an established structure which the failure of individual *agathoi* neither affected nor challenged; and his values and behaviour were entirely appropriate to the circumstances in which he lived.

Now, however, there are changes: the most radical being the invention of money. Money differs from land (or cattle or other bartered goods, which may be exchanged while the basis of wealth remains land) in several important respects: it may be acquired by a variety of means, means which are available to others besides the traditional landowning class; though evidently the amount of metal from which money may be manufactured in any society at any time is finite and limited, it may be increased in a manner, and to an extent, which would be quite impossible in the case of the society's holding of land; it is not perishable in the same way as is much agricultural produce; and it renders possible many types of financial transaction and enterprise not possible in a barter-economy. These factors are of themselves likely to throw into confusion a society of the Homeric type, and pose many problems of the kind to be discussed in this chapter; and other, linked, changes were taking place simultaneously. Important among these was the greater concentration of population in cities, a change which must in itself cause difficulties if Homeric values persist: a Homeric *agathos* requires considerable room to manœuvre, and would be a difficult next-door neighbour.

B. Hesiod: an *Agathos* in decline?

Hesiod's *Works and Days*, a poem of ethical and agricultural advice composed about 700, presents to us clearly the plight of Hesiod's own family in this new world, a world in which land can be bought and sold (341). Hesiod's father had been a resident in Aeolic Cyme, and had evidently fallen on hard times there: Hesiod reminds his brother Perses (630 ff.) how their father used to trade by sea, since he lacked *bios esthlos*, a good livelihood. Hesiod does not state explicitly that the family had become less prosperous, and one might argue that they had always been poor, and were availing themselves of the new economic opportunities to improve their fortunes by trade. Events, as Hesiod records them, however, suggest that the family was moving downwards in the social and economic scale. Being apparently unsuccessful as a merchant, Hesiod's father brought the family to Boeotia, and acquired—presumably by purchase—a farm at Ascra, in the foothills of Mt. Helicon, a place 'bad in winter, grievous in summer, and good at no time' (640). After their father's death, Perses, according to Hesiod,[1] took an unfairly large share of the inheritance, in whose possession he seems to have been confirmed by the 'lords', whose functions, as in Homer, included hearing such disputes. Hesiod hints that Perses may have used bribery; but he also addresses Perses thus (27 ff.):

> Perses . . . do not let the strife that takes pleasure in harm incline your spirit away from work, while you stare, and listen to the quarrels of the *agorā*.[2]

Hesiod, it seems, is not merely rebuking Perses for going to court in the matter of their own dispute; he is rebuking him also for spending his time in the *agora*, in the town, that is, away from the fields rather than occupying himself as one in his financial situation should, with the work of his own farm, his own *oikos*, in his case a unit too small to have sufficient servants to whom the work could be entrusted. This suggests that Perses, and Hesiod, belong to a family which has previously enjoyed much greater leisure, has been in fact a family of *agathoi*, and that whereas Hesiod himself has come to terms with the new life of practical farming enjoined upon them by their failing fortunes, Perses himself still longs for the leisure of the town. If this is so, the *Works and Days* throws an interesting light on one aspect of the problems of any erstwhile *agathos* who was succumbing to the buffets of the new economic storms. Hesiod's advice—the ethical advice, in particular—is then not directed to those who had always been humble

---

[1] Hesiod may have invented the dispute (and Perses) as a convenient means of presenting his ideas; but the wider situation with which he is concerned is evidently real.

[2] The court was held in the *agora*, the 'place of assembly'.

peasants, for these can surely never have needed to be told that 'Work is no disgrace; it is idleness that is a disgrace' (311). Such a small farmer had never had any choice in the matter: he was not an *agathos*, anyway, so that his way of life was *kakotes*, and so a disgrace, perforce. It was those whose previous expectations had been quite different, those whose life had been one of *arete*, which in peacetime prominently included the enjoyment of leisure, or at least more leisure than the majority of their fellow-Greeks, who needed Hesiod's consolation and advice. Doubtless the situation of Hesiod and Perses was not uncommon at the time: the consolation and advice—and the practical agricultural hints—were needed.

Hesiod wishes to deter Perses from aping the way of life of the *agathos* while his resources are insufficient; but naturally he too wishes for *arete*, which always commended the qualities which any Greek regarded as most important. But for *arete*, as understood at this period, more wealth is necessary than Hesiod—or Perses—possessed. Hesiod's exhortation to Perses (286 ff.) should be seen in this light:

> To you, foolish Perses, I will give good advice. *Kakotes* you may readily have in abundance. The way to it is smooth, and it dwells near at hand. But the immortal gods have set sweat in the way of attaining *arete*; and a path leads to it that is long and steep, and rough too at first; but when one reaches the summit, then *arete* is easy to possess, though before it was difficult.

Arete furnishes a leisured life; but a life without effort will never bring *arete* to the poor man, for whom, a *kakos*, only *kakotes* is to be had easily (308 ff.):

> It is by work that men gain many flocks and become wealthy; and by working they become much more *philos* (dearer) to the immortals. Work is no disgrace, it is idleness that is a disgrace. If you work, soon will the idle man envy you as you grow wealthy; and *arete* and fame accompany wealth. Since your lot is what it is, it is more *agathon* (beneficial) to work, if you will turn your misguided thoughts and desires away from other people's property to your work, and attend to your livelihood as I instruct you.

25

Phocylides, a poet of the mid sixth century, puts the point more succinctly (fr. 10):

> Seek a livelihood, and *arete* when your livelihood is secure.

Hesiod continues (317 ff.):

> *Aidos* is not beneficial when it attends upon a needy man— *aidos* which both greatly harms and prospers men. *Aidos* will lead you to poverty, *tharsos* (confidence, boldness) to wealth.

This is not the usually accepted translation of the last three lines, but it is possible, and gives a coherence to the thought which is not otherwise apparent. The lines resemble Telemachus' words in Homer referring to the disguised Odysseus (*Odyssey* XVII, 345 ff.):

> Take and give this to the stranger, and tell him to go about and beg of all the suitors in turn; for *aidos* is not *agathē* (beneficial) when it attends upon a needy man.

Works and Days 317 is an echo of the Homeric line, or more probably of a popular proverb which is the source of both; and this supports the translation of 317 that I have offered here. The situation is this: an *agathos* has no need to do, and should be ashamed to do, many things which a *kakos* must do; for example, as in Homer, beg, or, as here in Hesiod, work with his hands.[1] In both cases one whose status is that of a *kakos* is being exhorted to have no thoughts of the *aidos* which befits an *agathos*. Such *aidos* can only harm the *kakos*. For the *agathos*, of course, *aidos* is one of the restraints which prevents him from doing what is *aischron*, the mark of a *kakos*; and in so doing it benefits him, for it is less advantageous to be a *kakos* than to be an *agathos*. Hence Hesiod's 318 and the need for such lines as 317 and *Odyssey* XVII, 347: *aidos* may be beneficial or harmful according to one's circumstances. Once again, Perses is exhorted to forget about the standards of the *agathos* while he

---

[1] In the *Odyssey* it is Odysseus in his folk-tale aspect, not Odysseus the Homeric warrior, who builds a raft (V, 243 ff.) and made his own bedstead (XXIII, 178 ff.); and it is Odysseus disguised as a beggar who proclaims his skill with a sickle (XVIII, 366 ff.).

remains impoverished, particularly where these very standards will prevent him from attaining to *arete*.

But may the *kakos*, in so far as he is aiming at the attainment or the recovery of *arete*, cast off all restraints and do anything and everything, be in fact a *panourgos*, literally 'one who does everything', one of the Greek words for 'rogue'? *Arete* is the goal, the unquestioned end; what restraints are available to limit the choice of means, to ensure that the pursuit of *arete* will be, for example, just, as Hesiod certainly holds that it should be? What inducement can be offered to Perses, or to anyone else, to co-operate justly with the other members of his society, when the society accepts these values?

If prosperity is the goal, then the most effective way of commending the less-valued justice is to ensure that the unjust do not prosper, or at all events that it is believed that the unjust do not prosper. At 265 f. Hesiod says:

> He who does *kaka* (harm) to another does *kaka* to himself, and a *kakē* (harmful) plan is *kakistē* (most harmful) for the person who made the plan.

While at 213 ff. we have:

> But, Perses, listen to what is just and do not foster *hubris* (excess); for *hubris* is *kake* (harmful) to a poor man. Even an *esthlos* cannot easily bear its burden when he meets with *ātai* (disasters). The more *agathe* (beneficial to oneself) road is to go past on the other side towards justice; for justice beats *hubris* when she comes to the end of the course. But the fool learns this only when he has suffered.

How the harm-doers are harmed in 265 f. is unclear. Zeus is mentioned in 267; but 267 seems to be the beginning of a new paragraph; and the confidence that Zeus will punish is in any case not very high in 269 ff. Hesiod seems to be saying that harmful action in some way of its own accord brings harmful consequences to the agent. Whether such harmful consequences are 'in the nature of things', or the result of human reprisals, is unclear. In 213 ff., the passage as quoted suggests that gods are not involved in ensuring that the *hubris* of the *esthlos* is not beneficial to him. 'Even an *esthlos* cannot easily

27

bear its burden'; but the gods could bring an *esthlos* to disaster as readily as they could bring low anyone else: the 'even' and the contrast with *deilos* seem not relevant if the gods are in the poet's mind. Hesiod's point appears to be that the *esthlos* is liable to *atai*, and that if he suffered one his previous *hubris* would be not beneficial to him, presumably because other human beings would then take reprisals. In 213 ff. there seems no suggestion whatever that *hubris* leads *necessarily* to *ātē*,[1] whether by itself or as a result of divine action.

The *esthlos* might be particularly subject to disasters in a time of economic change; but for the wronged simply to sit and wait for such a disaster is unconsoling: if neither he nor the *esthlos* think that anything but chance will bring the disaster, then the more successful the *esthlos* becomes, the less he will fear the possibility that he may fall.[2] Hesiod in fact goes on (225 ff.):

> But they who give straight judgments to strangers and to the people of the land, and do not depart from justice— their city flourishes, and the people prosper in it. Peace, the nurse of children, is throughout their land, and Zeus who sees far and wide never decrees grievous war against them. Neither famine nor *ate* ever consorts with men who give straight judgments; with festivity they cultivate the fields that are their care. For them the earth bears abundant livelihood, and on the mountains the oak bears acorns upon the top, and in the middle bees. Their woolly sheep are heavy with fleeces, and the women bear children like their parents. They enjoy abundance of *agatha* (good things) continually, and do not travel on ships, for the grain-giving earth bears fruit for them.

These lines resemble *Odyssey* XIX, 107 ff. Hesiod's list is fuller, and it is noteworthy that 'not having to go to sea' is one of the promised blessings. He continues (238 ff.):

[1] Contrast pp. 29 f. and 85 f. below. *Ate* spans 'blindness' and disaster because, in a results-culture, a condition and its consequences are not distinguished.

[2] I shall discuss below the relationship between *hubris* and injustice. See pp. 84 ff.

But for those who practise *hubris* and harsh deeds, Zeus . . . ordains a punishment. Often even a whole city suffers because of a *kakos* who does wrong and contrives *atasthala* ('presumptuous' deeds). Upon the people the son of Cronos sends a mighty woe, plague and famine together; and the people perish, and their wives do not bear children, and their *oikoi* waste away, at the will of Olympian Zeus. And at another time the son of Cronos either destroys their wide army on their walls, or their ships on the sea.

Zeus is to punish *hubris*; and his concern with such punishment now seems more widespread than in Homer. In Homer Zeus may be associated with the punishment of *hubris*—or rather, of some *hubris*. When *hubris* is exercised towards the beggar, the wanderer, the suppliant, the guest, it may be punished (*Odyssey* XVI, 416 ff., XVII, 482 ff., XXIII, 62 ff.): it is for this reason that the gods go around in the likeness of strangers from other lands; and the *hubris* of the suitors, when hoped-for punishment is associated with it, consists in the manner in which they treated strangers who came to the palace. Such acts of *hubris* the gods may punish of their own accord. Telemachus evaluates differently the likely attitude of the gods to what the suitors are doing to him (*Odyssey* III, 205 ff.):

Would that the gods would give me sufficient power to *tinesthai* ('punish') for their grievous wrongs the suitors who *hubrizein* and contrive wicked deeds. But the gods have not granted me such *olbos* (good fortune), neither to me nor to my father; as it is we must endure.

Telemachus is not a beggar, a wanderer, a suppliant or a guest; and he has little confidence that the gods will punish the suitors' *hubris* towards him.

Hesiod seems more hopeful that Zeus will punish *hubris* more widely interpreted: Zeus appears now to be concerned with more than harm done to beggars, wanderers, suppliants and guests. Furthermore, 238 ff. may indicate another increase in range. In *Odyssey* XIX, 107 ff. the well-being of the society is associated, most unusually for Homer, with the justice of the king. To this belief Hesiod has added explicit mention of

29

Zeus (Homer's king is 'god-fearing', 109, but the identity of the god is not mentioned) in 229 and 239; but *kakos* in 240 seems a much more significant addition. The word is customarily rendered 'bad' here; but words of this group in Hesiod, and long afterwards, still commend competitive excellences and decry their absence. *Esthlos* in 214 commends prosperity and social status; and to understand *kakos* here as decrying their absence makes admirable sense. Zeus now watches over not only the *hubris* of the *agathoi* but also that of the *kakoi*; and the *hubris* even of a *kakos* may cause the ruin of the whole city. (The use that can be made of the idea of the *hubris* of *kakoi* in other circumstances will appear below.)[1]

If these beliefs are accepted, they are a powerful inducement not merely to be just oneself but to take an interest in the general justice of one's society; and since famines and plagues occur, armies are defeated and ships lost at sea, events in which the ancient Greeks saw the hand of deities at work, the beliefs may be accepted: it is evident that not all the inhabitants of the city are unjust, yet the gods are sending general disaster. In so far as the belief is accepted, it renders justice as important as competitive *arete* in securing the success of the city's army; but the link is much less evident than in the case of *arete* manifested in actual fighting, and depends on the actions of a Zeus whose justice, though hoped for by Hesiod, is rendered doubtful by much else that is narrated of him in myth. Hesiod himself, as we shall see, is not without doubts.

Hesiod also tries to suggest—most unusually for an early Greek—that cruel behaviour is unsuited to human beings as such. At 202 ff. he relates the story of the hawk and the nightingale, prefacing it with the statement that he will now tell a tale which the rulers will understand themselves. At first we may find it difficult to understand it ourselves, on the assumption that the intention is to deter the ruler from injustice, since the outcome of the tale is the following speech made by the hawk to the nightingale (207 ff.):

[1] Pp. 84 ff., especially 87. Hesiod himself seems to have acts of injustice mostly in mind in writing of *hubris* here; but we shall see that the implications may be much more complex.

Miserable creature, why do you lament? One who is far stronger than you has you in his grip, and you shall go wherever I take you, singer though you be; and I shall either make you my dinner or let you go, as I choose. He is foolish who tries to resist the stronger, for he is bereft of victory and suffers woes in addition to *aischeă* (disgrace).

Now the achievement of victory and the avoidance of the disgrace of defeat is more important than justice in early Greece (and in these lines there is no mention of justice at all); and the situation here described is undoubtedly *aischron* for the nightingale, not for the hawk. Being ourselves accustomed to parables in which the creatures or objects mentioned are merely symbols for what is signified, and in which we direct, and are expected to direct, our attention to what is signified,[1] we may simply see Hesiod in the guise of the nightingale, the sweet singer, and treat the parable in isolation; whereupon Hesiod seems to be conceding that his situation is *aischron* and that it would be foolish to try to improve it. However, later in the poem (274 ff.) Hesiod explicitly contrasts what is appropriate for animals, birds and fishes, with behaviour which is appropriate for human beings:

Perses, lay up these things in your heart and listen to what is just, and forget violence altogether. For Zeus has established this law for men, that fishes and wild beasts and winged birds should eat one another, for they have no *dikē* (justice) among them; but to mankind he gave *dike*, which proves to be much the most *agathe* (beneficial). Zeus gives *olbos* (prosperity) to anyone who knows what is just and is ready to declare it; but the family of the false witness . . . is left in obscurity, while that of him who swears truly becomes more *agathe* for the future.

Human beings alone have *dike*, which is a gift from Zeus that distinguishes them from animals in general; and it is also good for them, beneficial, which links this passage to the other means of commending justice and the other co-operative excellences.

[1] When reading the Parable of the Sower, for example, we do not usually consider likely wheat yields in first-century A.D. Palestine.

To be convinced, one must of course believe that *dike*, and co-operative excellences generally, will in fact be more profitable for oneself than simply exerting every means in one's power to achieve as much material success as possible. Hesiod is under no illusions about the priorities, as may be seen (*Works and Days* 267 ff.):

> The eye of Zeus, that sees and observes all things, sees these things too, if he wishes, and it does not escape his notice what kind of justice is this that the city keeps within it. Now, therefore, may neither I nor my son be *dikaios* among men, for it is *kakon* (disadvantageous) to be *dikaios* if he who is more *adikos* is to have the greater right. But I think that counsellor Zeus will not yet accomplish this.

Hesiod himself seems to believe that justice will prevail, as the last line quoted indicates. At all events—observe 'not yet'—he believes this to be true of the present stage of cosmic development. The 'five races' myth, however, indicates (109 ff.) that the state of affairs is not only bad but is to get worse; an attitude of mind doubtless attractive to many in a period of social and economic turmoil, but most of all to one who has suffered social and economic disadvantage. But in general the belief that the just man always prospers might be rather difficult to sustain at such a time, as other writers to be discussed in this chapter indicate.

There are other problems. As we have seen, Hesiod tells Perses, and anyone else who will listen, that no disgrace is occasioned by hard work. However, in adjuring them to cast off *aidos* he says that it is not beneficial to a poor man, not that it is an inappropriate response, in the sense of a response not justified by the most powerful values of the society, for any erstwhile *agathos* who must work. Since *arete* is the highest condition, commended by the most powerful value-words of the society, and since the life of *arete* requires leisure, how can anyone who regards himself as an *agathos*, as Perses doubtless still regarded himself, not feel *aidos* at having to work? Anyone so situated would be unlikely to agree that work is no disgrace. Those who were poor, *kakoi*, in the static Homeric society might merely feel resignation, for they could never aspire to

32

arete anyway, and knew that work was an inescapable condition of their lives; those who were *kakoi* and now found
themselves in a more mobile society might well adopt the
attitude of Phocylides in the line quoted above—get yourself
a livelihood first and then think about *arete*. Hesiod himself
takes such a view, and is commending it to Perses; but the
dilemma of the erstwhile *agathos* can be understood.

Hesiod's analysis of the needs of society also poses problems.
He writes (11 ff.):

> So, it turns out, there was not only one kind of strife, but
> two. One of them a man would praise when he understood
> the matter, while the other is blameworthy; and they are
> quite different in character. The one fosters hurtful war
> and *dēris* (conflict), and is cruel.

The other, however, is much more beneficial to men; for she
stirs up even the shiftless individual to work (21 ff.):

> For a man grows eager to work when he sees another,
> a richer man, who bestirs himself to plough and plant and
> put his *oikos* in good order; and neighbour vies with neigh-
> bour as he hastens eagerly after wealth. This strife is *agathe*
> (beneficial) for men. And potter is angry with potter and
> carpenter with carpenter, and beggar is envious of beggar
> and minstrel of minstrel.

The latter passage sketches a vigorous competitive society
in which the small farmer and the craftsman may, by their
efforts, attain to wealth and so, presumably, to *arete* if they
are sufficiently successful. (The further effects of this will
appear below.) This strife is beneficial: whether to the
individual alone or to society as a whole Hesiod does not make
clear, but he evidently agrees with Samuel Johnson that no
man is more innocently employed than in getting money.
Even this competition, as Hesiod realises, sets man against
man; but he seems unconcerned. The nature of 'good strife'
seems clear; but what of bad strife? It is not merely war, for
(27 ff.) Perses' litigation is an example of it; and *deris* is not
simply 'war'. *Odyssey* XXIV, 513 ff. is illuminating. Laertes,
Odysseus' father, is delighted by Telemachus' assurance to

33

Odysseus that he will not shame, *kataischūnein*, the family by fighting inadequately in the coming struggle with the parents of the suitors whom they have killed:

> What a day is this, dear gods! Much do I rejoice. My son and my grandson are engaged in *deris* about *arete*.

In the context, it is evident that *deris* is not the coming fight, but the competition between Telemachus and Odysseus; and it is a competition for *arete*. In his description of the 'bad strife', Hesiod presents *deris* as a result or concomitant of that strife; but *deris* is just as closely linked with any kind of strife. The difference is that Hesiod presents *deris* as the result of one kind of strife, prosperity as the result of the other; but of course in the minds of those engaging in them, their own prosperity and *arete* is the goal whether of war, litigation or business competition; and Hesiod cannot deny that *deris* accompanies the 'good strife', for the anger of potter with potter and the envy of beggar for beggar is *deris* too. Hesiod may himself believe that one kind of strife is beneficial to the individual, the other not, and he might be able to distinguish inter-city warfare conceptually from the rest (though this too is strife for *arete*),[1] and to gain agreement that such strife is bad for the individual. However, despite his insistence that the two strifes are 'quite different in character', Hesiod does not attempt to draw any distinction between them save their results; and both in fact aim at personal prosperity and *arete*, and are associated with conflict and competition. One aspect of 'bad strife' is litigation in the manner of a Perses; but in the light of early Greek values, the only way of demonstrating to Perses the 'badness' of the 'bad strife' of litigation and the 'goodness' of the 'good strife' of the farmer is by showing that the individual engaging in 'bad strife' will suffer reduced, not increased, prosperity as the result of such strife: the only method of showing that any path to the goal of *arete* is not choiceworthy is to demonstrate that it does not in fact lead there. Particularly at a time of social and economic turmoil, the proof might be difficult in the light of observable facts.

The context has changed since Homer; but the basic prob-

[1] See Tyrtaeus, p. 35.

lem posed by the nature and structure of Greek values has
not.

C. TYRTAEUS: *Arete* AND THE WARRIOR

For Hesiod, the problems of life are economic; and consequently *arete* in his eyes commends, of the whole Homeric
complex, predominantly wealth and its concomitant leisure.
Tyrtaeus, the seventh-century Spartan war-poet, and traditionally the Spartan general in the second Messenian war,
finds his society in a situation that makes different demands,
and simplifies Homeric *arete* in a different manner. He declares
(12, 1 ff.) that he would not reckon a man as of any account
because of the *arete* of his feet, or for wrestling, or for a number
of other qualities which were *aretai* in the customary evaluation of the day. Even if a man had every ground for fame but
fierce valour, Tyrtaeus would not grant that he had *arete*:

> For a man does not become *agathos* in war if he should not
> hold firm when he sees bloody carnage and thrust at the
> enemy from close at hand. This is *arete*.

Since it is *arete*, it is also most *agathon* and most *kalon* for a
young man to win (12, 13 f.); and such an *agathos*, if successful
in battle, would be unlikely to disagree. But in another poem
(10, 1 f.) Tyrtaeus also maintains that it is *kalon* for an *agathos*
to die fighting bravely for his city; and this, *kalon* or no—and
the expression seems novel—is evidently not *agathon*, beneficial,
for the *agathos* himself. Now over most of the range of *arete*,
agathos and *kalon*, it is more advantageous to be *agathos*, to do
what is *kalon*, to display *arete*, than to be *kakos*, to do what is
aischron and display *kakotes* or *kakiā*, for the one group commends success and prosperity, the other decries failure and
adversity; but clearly to die, even to die bravely in battle
fighting for one's city, is *kakon*, harmful, for oneself. It is, of
course, as Tyrtaeus says in 12, 15, a common *esthlon*, benefit,
for the city and all the people; but this is a group bigger than
one's own *oikos*, and nothing we have seen so far gives any
motivation for the *agathos* to risk dying himself on behalf of
such a larger group; and it is clear that Tyrtaeus realises the
problem. In poem 10 he not only says that it is *kalon* to die

35

fighting bravely, as an *agathos*, for one's city, he also characterises the alternative (2 ff.):

> But to leave one's own city and rich fields, and beg, is the most painful of all, as one wanders with mother, aged father, small children and wedded wife. For he finds hostile those among whom he comes in his need and hateful penury, and he *aischūnein* his family, and belies his splendid appearance; and all manner of *atīmiā* (absence of property, rights and status) and *kakotes* accompanies him. So, if no regard or *aidos* or respect or pity is felt for a wanderer, let us fight bravely for this land and our children, not sparing our lives.

It may be *kakon* for oneself to die fighting bravely; but much greater *kaka* to oneself and one's *oikos* result from defeat or flight; and Tyrtaeus reminds the warrior also (11, 11 ff.) that one is much more likely to be killed while running away than while fighting bravely.

Thus far there are few problems of values: one must fight on behalf of the city, for if the whole city falls the lot of each citizen is terrible; and it is *kalon* to risk death in such a cause. But if the *agathos* risks his life on behalf of the larger unit in this manner, then the inhabitants of the larger unit, the citizens in general, must surely recognize his services in some way if he fights bravely, displays *arete*, does what is *kalon* and is not killed, but lives. If he is killed, the recompense is fame, for himself and his family in future generations, a fame that will never die (12, 32):[1] even in his grave he is immortal, in memory, that is to say, the only kind of immortality hoped for by most ancient Greeks of whom we have any knowledge. If he is not killed, he is assured of *time* and respect from young and old; even in old age he shines out among the citizens, and no-one wishes to hurt him in respect either of *aidos* or justice.

Here once again we have a situation which will long persist in later Greece. For a variety of reasons, some citizens are more capable of making a contribution to the defence of the

[1] When a warrior has been killed, of course, one must insist that Ares spares not the *agathos*, but the *kakos*, Anacreon 150 and cf. 149.

city than are others. It is not merely a question of being courageous and having a strong right arm: one must, in a society such as this, purchase one's own armour; and so, as in Homer, it is only the more wealthy that can be effectively armed. A wider distribution of wealth in society now begins to make the hoplite phalanx possible as a means of defence, and ensures that there are more *agathoi*; but these still form only a small proportion of society, and their contribution to the defence and well-being of the city is manifestly greater than that of the citizens in general. As Tyrtaeus informs us, they have a greater claim to the esteem of the citizen-body as a whole. The advantages that they enjoy are not described here in detail, and must have varied from time to time and place to place; but it is more evidently relevant to the stability and prosperity of the city in circumstances such as these that one should be brave and well-armed than that one should be just; so that the successful *agathos* may under some circumstances be able to ask society that it be willing to overlook his injustices. Of course, if society or the *agathos* himself believes that disaster, heaven-sent, will punish his injustice and reduce his *arete* he may be deterred from being unjust; but this situation poses difficult problems, as we shall see clearly in other writers. Sparta escaped or mitigated many of the economic problems mentioned in this chapter by shutting the state off from economic development, a policy rendered possible by the conquest of Messenia and the acquisition of a large helot population; but other cities experienced the problem which arises from evaluations such as those of Tyrtaeus, for the need of successful defence was always pressing; and when the need was met, it gave the *agathos* a claim against society.

D. THEOGNIS: *Agathoi* AND *Kakoi* IN CONFLICT

The collection of elegiac poems preserved under the name of Theognis, the bulk of which appears to belong to the sixth century, reflects very clearly the stresses and strains upon values and behaviour imposed by the invention of money, with consequent increased social mobility and economic opportunity. The poems record the different attitudes of the *agathos*, or the number of different *agathoi*,[1] who wrote them, in face of the lost certainties of the old order and the baffling complexities of the new. 227 ff. are directly evoked by the economic conditions:

> There is no clear limit for wealth established among mankind; for those who now have the greatest riches among us strive to double them. Who could satisfy them all? Possessions turn to folly for mortal men, and disaster comes from folly, which attends now upon one man, now on another, when Zeus sends it upon them in their misery.

The limited land-based wealth of a small city-state is now supplemented from other, less clearly limited, sources. The old *agathos*, landed aristocrat, may be reluctant to make money by trade or similar means; and he is certainly no longer the only person who can do so. As a result, those who were *kakoi* under the old system may become prosperous and successful. This strains the system of values. In the Homeric world, the qualities commended by *agathos*, *arete* and similar words were always found together in the very small upper class. Now they are separated: one may be wealthy even though one does not belong to the landowners, and some landowners are evidently, as Theognis indicates, less wealthy than before; and it is clearly of importance to decide who are now the *agathoi*, what, that is, are the criteria of *arete*. Since *agathos* and *arete* are the most powerful words of commendation, the question is an emotive one.

The question is also difficult; and it is not surprising that the Theognid poems are not agreed upon the answer. One may write (183 ff.):

> In the case of rams, asses and horses, Cyrnus, we seek creatures of good pedigree, and each man wishes to get offspring from *agathoi* beasts; but an *esthlos* man does not hesitate to marry the *kake* daughter of a *kakos* father, if the father gives him many possessions. Nor does a woman refuse to be the wife of a *kakos*, provided he is wealthy. No; she prefers a wealthy husband rather than an *agathos*. For they

[1] 894 seems datable to about 580, 773–82 to about 490. 'Theognis' appears to be a collection of the works of several poets.

38

honour possessions; and an *esthlos* has married from *kakon* stock, and a *kakos* from *agathon* stock. Wealth has thrown lineage into confusion. So do not be surprised, son of Polypaüs, that the lineage of the citizens is being dimmed; it is because *esthla* are being mixed with *kaka*.

In Homer, of course, wealth was important in matrimony; but since only *agathoi* possessed wealth, the criterion served to link the households of *agathoi*, wealthy landowners. Money, gained from trade, has changed all that: many who do not belong to the small circle of the old *agathoi* are now wealthy, and wealthy enough to marry into that small circle, some of whose members are evidently prepared to accept them.

The new successful group is unlikely to be willing to continue to be termed *kakos*: after all, *arete* commends success, and they are successful, as even the writers of the Theognid corpus sometimes acknowledge: the men who used to wander in goatskins outside the city walls (57 ff.).

> Now are *agathoi*; and those who were before *esthloi* are now *deiloi*.

'*Deiloi*' naturally enough, if wealth and success are the criteria, and the old aristocrats are now less successful. These must resent their new obscurity: the bitterness of 699 f., 'for the majority of men there is only one *arete*—to be wealthy' is evident. The old aristocrats will not lightly concede their claim to be *agathoi* (865 ff.):

> To many useless men the god gives *esthlos* (good) prosperity . . .; but the great fame of *arete* shall never die, for a spearman preserves his native land and his city.

Again (315 ff.):

> Many *kakoi* are rich and many *agathoi* are poor; but we will not take wealth in exchange for our *arete*; for the one remains with a man always, but possessions pass from one to another.

Fighting ability and high birth are among the qualities traditionally commended by *arete*, and the former may claim to be basic. Evidently the *agathos* of 865 ff. is still able to equip himself as a warrior, and the new rich are not so equipped, despite their wealth.[1] The old *agathoi* have powerful reasons for not wishing the new rich to be armed: firstly because their own defence of the society constitutes a great part of their claim to be *agathoi*, and would furnish any others who so defended the society with a similar claim; and secondly the competitive nature of *arete* enjoins upon the individual that he should succeed by whatever means; and to arm the newly successful, or rather to permit them to be armed, would furnish them with means of taking political power by force. The different groups and classes in Megara are not engaged in a discussion about semantics and the use of language merely; they are competing for prestige and power, and their being termed *agathoi* is the acknowledgement that the one or the other party has succeeded in obtaining, or retaining, them.

Poverty in itself will prevent the *agathos* from playing an effective part in society (173 ff.):

> Poverty subdues the *agathos* most of all, more than hoary old age and ague . . . for every man who is overwhelmed by poverty can neither say nor do anything, and his tongue is fettered.

In early Greece in general an individual is valued for the effective contribution he can make in war and in public life. Anyone who can make no such contribution 'is nothing'—a complaint uttered by the aged (for an example in the later fifth century, see Aristophanes, *Acharnians* 681). Poverty, says the writer, is worse than old age for the *agathos*. He is accustomed to be effective in the public sphere on the basis of his wealth: poverty, depriving him of effectiveness and consequently of prestige, leaves him unable to speak (in public), for he would no longer be valued; and the new rich may aspire to the influence he has lost.

Much of the Theognid corpus presents to us a picture of a society in turmoil, as the old *agathoi* and the new rich contend for positions of power and the value-terms that accompany

[1] The wider distribution of wealth in society made possible the development of the hoplite phalanx (above, p. 37), since more citizens could afford to purchase armour; but the traditional *agathoi* may well not have always welcomed the new situation, or have wished

them. It should never be forgotten that these value-terms are the most powerful in the society and do indeed commend the human being at his best, as the society understands the matter; and that the success and prosperity which these terms commend are the goal of life: anything else will take a subordinate place, as a means to the desired end. The individual *agathos* seems to have been uncertain how to maximise his success, as he might well be in the circumstances. The poems make it clear that old alignments and alliances among *agathoi* tended to break down under the strain: Cyrnus, to whom many of the poems are addressed, is repeatedly (29 ff., 101 ff., 105 ff. etc.) exhorted to have nothing to do with the *kakoi*. *Kakos* evidently decries those of 'low birth', and of them those who have become prosperous: Cyrnus is forming alliances, *philiai*—or the poet fears that he may form alliances—with the new rich. (When *agathoi* are accused of making *philoi* of *kakoi*, the situation is sometimes that a powerful individual is seeking to make himself tyrant by championing the cause of the poor, the *kakoi*;[1] but though the writer of some of these poems fears lest a tyrant may arise (39 ff.), Cyrnus seems not to be directly associated with this: it is rather that discord and disloyalty among the *agathoi* may give a tyrant his chance.)

The poems in general reflect a state of affairs in which *philiai*, friendships, alliances, were changing and breaking down all the time, and in which no *agathos* (and no *kakos*) could trust his neighbour or his old *philos* very far. Such a state of affairs is clearly unlikely to lead to stable prosperity for anyone, and the Theognid poems contain a number in which prudence and moderation in politics are urged as a means to *arete*. For example (335 f.):

> Do not be over zealous. Moderation in all things is best, and in this way, Cyrnus, you shall have *arete*, which is difficult to attain.

---

to accept spearmen from families that had traditionally been *kakoi*; and if some of the new rich traded abroad in person, the mobility of their lives would render it less likely that they would be present when defence was needed.

[1] See below, pp. 69 ff.

We should not assume that Theognis is advocating an Aristotelian mean, or that *arete* has come to commend moderation, less success than one might have; the writer means that the most success, *arete*, that one can get is attainable only by moderation.

There is one quatrain in the Theognid poems which goes astonishingly further than this (145 ff.):

> Be willing to be a pious man and dwell with little wealth
> rather than be wealthy with possessions unjustly acquired.
> The whole of *arete* is summed up in *dikaiosunē*: every man,
> Cyrnus, is *agathos* if he is *dikaios*.

The couplet must have amazed the writer's contemporaries; for he is not claiming that one may be termed *agathos* only if (whatever other conditions may be necessary in addition) one is *dikaios*, which, though far from Homeric, could be fitted into Homeric values. He is claiming that *anyone* who is *dikaios* is *agathos*; and this smashes the whole framework of Homeric values. What has happened seems fairly clear. The writer is living in a society in a state of economic and political turmoil, reflected in the problem of the application of value-terms which we have noticed. Forced by this crisis to consider more carefully the reasons for the application of these terms—which are, of course, that the *agathos* makes more of a contribution to the well-being and stability of society than anyone else—he has come to the conclusion that what makes the most contribution to the stability and well-being of society is *dikaiosune*, the quiet co-operation of one citizen with another. At this early period —and indeed later—such an insight is likely to occur only at a time of crisis; but since the criteria of *arete* are at this time under scrutiny, it is easier for the writer to claim that it is the co-operative excellences which make the most contribution and to annex to them the words *agathos* and *arete*. In so doing he is giving the *dikaios* the highest of commendation, and endowing him, and *dikaiosune*, with the overtones of splendour, position and success, all of which, as the result of traditional and common usage, are part of the flavour of *agathos*. The man who is *dikaios*, claims this writer, possesses all these in the true sense, as no-one else does.

This quatrain results from more thought than the others quoted above. Were it accepted, it would have the immediate result that, *dikaiosune* and *arete* being identical, there would be no need any longer to justify the pursuit of *dikaiosune*, for the pursuit of *arete* is a desirable end. However, there is little sign —and much indication to the contrary—that such judgments as this had any effect. Aristotle in the *Nicomachean Ethics* terms the couplet a proverb (1129b29); but there is little sign of any effect of it in extant literature for long after the time of Theognis. *Arete* remains essentially, as it has been, a matter of competitive success; and that being so, some means of ensuring that *dikaiosune* and the co-operative excellences generally are necessary to the securing of *arete* is required. If human aid fails, the help of heaven must be sought. The unjust must be punished; and since belief in a punishment after death is not characteristic of this period, the punishment must come visibly in this life. Now at a time of great social and economic upheaval, when great fortunes are being made—and lost— when individuals are rising in the world with dramatic sudden- ness—and falling too, for the way of the early business man cannot have been easy—and the old wealthy are declining, it is likely to be the case that many either actually prosper by injustice or are deemed to have done so, particularly by those, the old *agathoi*, to whose detriment it is that anyone other than themselves should succeed. Accordingly it is likely that many will be held to have committed great injustices and neverthe- less died in their beds successful and prosperous.

At this period, however, a solution is still at least theoretic- ally possible. At some time in the dark age of Greece there appeared a belief, which is found also in other cultures, that the children, or subsequent generations—five is the maximum recorded, when Croesus (Herodotus I, 91) pays the penalty for the misdeeds of his ancestor Gyges—may be punished for the injustices their parents or more remote forebears have committed. The attitude is readily comprehensible in a largely agricultural society. The plot of land cultivated by the family furnishes the family's livelihood. It is inherited, in earliest times inalienable, and even when it may be sold the sale is likely to be regarded as a disaster, since for most Greeks only

43

economic failure could motivate it. Accordingly, the plot of land persists and is of vital importance, while those who cultivate it change from generation to generation. In such circumstances the individual is likely to be reckoned as of little importance in comparison with the continuing plot of land and its continuing family.

Now this belief furnishes an explanation in ethical terms for the good or bad fortune of any individual: if he is just and prospers, or unjust and suffers adversity, it is what he deserves; and the co-operative excellences are supported. If he is unjust and prospers, a descendant will suffer; and if he is just and suffers adversity, he is being punished for the misdeeds of an ancestor. The belief that one's own injustice may harm a descendant may act as an effective restraint, not only from family feeling, but also from the desire to have descendants to make offerings to one's shade; but the possibility that one may be just and yet suffer adversity presses hard, and the more so the more the individual feels a sense of his own importance. While the plot of land is paramount, and divine punishment takes the form of (otherwise inexplicable) crop failure, it may be accepted as a fact of human existence: one passage in the Theognid corpus merely records the belief (205 ff.). But at the very time when the belief is first attested in literature its justice is vehemently questioned. The gods should see to it that if the wrongdoer delights in *hubris*, with no regard for the gods, he (735 ff.)

> Should straightway pay the penalty for the *kaka* (harm) he has done, that the wrongful deeds of the father should not be *kakon* (harmful) to his children, and that the children of an unjust father who are themselves just . . . should not pay for the transgression of their father. . . . As it is, the man who does wrong escapes, and another man endures the *kakon* (harm) thereafter.

The individual is feeling his own importance: a circumstance presumably not unconnected with the fact that society has now more non-agricultural activities in which individual enterprise is more favoured, while the farmer himself has, in money, a less perishable commodity than any he has possessed before.

44

We must remember that *arete*, the highest expression of human existence, is manifested in the possession of the maximum of prosperity. To the attainment of *arete* other activities stand as means. If *for the individual* there is no necessary link between justice and prosperity, there must now be a strong temptation to pursue prosperity and *arete*, and chance the vagaries of divine retribution. Justice might well be accompanied by disaster, after all, if requital was needed for the misdeeds of some ancestor.

Nor, as is clear from this very passage, does it solve any problems for Theognis to term an action *hubris*: writers of this period do not believe that *hubris* is inevitably punished in the person of the wrongdoer himself. (Even Hesiod has his doubts.) Empirically observable circumstances must have furnished them with little inducement to do so.

Again, the gods are but intermittently just in Greek belief from Homer onwards; they may also give success and failure out of caprice; and the events of the sixth century must have done little to discourage such a belief. So we have (133 ff.):

> No-one, Cyrnus, is himself the cause of his disaster or gain. No; the gods are the givers of both these things to men. Nor does any man know as he works whether he is making for an *agathon* (beneficial) or *kakon* (hurtful) goal. For often when he thinks he will bring about a *kakon* end he brings about an *agathon*, and when he thinks he will bring about an *esthlon* end, he brings about a *kakon*. Nor does any man gain what he wishes; for the constraints of dire *amēchaniā* (perplexity) have him in their grasp. Vain are the practices of us mortal men, for we know nothing; but the gods accomplish all things in accordance with their desire.

Here there is no suggestion that success has any link with just behaviour; but success is the highest value, and if furnished by heaven can be supposed to argue that the gods are on one's side, at least for the moment; and for what higher can one pray? 653/4:

> May I be *eudaimōn* and *philos* (dear) to the immortal gods, Cyrnus; and I long for no other *arete*.

To be *eudaimon* is etymologically to have a favourable *daimōn*,

45

to have the gods on one's side; and it is used to denote and commend prosperity: what other *arete* does one need?

Accordingly, this additional problem and perplexity exists for the Greek of Theognis' day. If the gods fail to bring a prosperous and unjust individual to adversity, they are not merely failing to punish, they are positively favouring and showing their approval of him; and since the gods may be thought of as completely amoral bestowers of prosperity and adversity, there is all the more inducement to pursue by any available means whatever advantage offers itself.

The impression given by the Theognid poems is readily comprehensible in the light of what we know of Greece in the sixth century. It is not surprising that *amechania*, perplexity, a condition in which one is unable to achieve anything, should be so prevalent. Old *agathos* and new rich may well have been equally perplexed. At all events, the writer of 683 ff. can hold

> Many who are wealthy are ignorant; and others seek *ta kala* while oppressed by dire penury. *Amechania* sits by both groups; for lack of money constrains the one, lack of wits the other.

Presumably the traditional *agathoi* suffered the worse *amechania*. These are partisan poems; and though the new rich doubtless did not engage in *ta kala*, the ways of the traditional *agathoi*, in a manner likely to satisfy the traditional *agathoi* themselves, and though they would at first have been completely ignorant of law and politics, previously the domain of the traditional *agathoi*, the successful businessman is likely to have had both the desire and the energy to succeed in other fields. Civil strife cannot have been pleasant for either group; but the poems, viewing the events through the eyes of the traditional *agathoi*, leave little doubt that the new rich are succeeding, while the traditional *agathos* feels himself to be in a world from which all the familiar certainties have disappeared.

E. XENOPHANES AND SOLON:
Eunomia AND THE LAWGIVER

The writers of the Theognid corpus for the most part feel themselves unable to exercise any effective control over the economic, social and political development of their city, which they neither approve nor understand. Two other writers of the period, however, Xenophanes and Solon, look at the situation as lawgivers (*nomothetai*), actual or potential, who have a plan for action. Xenophanes in fact complains that he has the skill needed 'to fatten the treasure-houses of his city' (2, 22) but that it is not appreciated. If a man were a successful athlete he would receive all manner of honours and rewards[1] from his city, though (2, 11 ff.):

He is not worthy of it, as I am; for better than the strength of men and horses is my *sophiā* (wisdom).

Xenophanes regards himself as more worthy of reward than the successful athlete; for not even if a man excelled in all sports (2, 19):

Would his city be any the more in a state of *eunomiā* ('sound government').

Xenophanes' *sophia* is evidently a practical skill devoted to the production of *eunomia*, whose implications I shall discuss below, and to 'fattening the treasure-houses of the city'. Such a skill was clearly needed by Greek cities, whether or no they realised it.

Space does not permit a detailed discussion of the social, economic and political situation with which Solon was faced. It must suffice to say that many of the smaller farmers of early sixth-century Attica were in debt, whether to larger farmers or to other wealthy individuals, and many had been forced into the position of bondmen to their creditors. Solon by his reforms freed them, and by his political innovations spread the basis of political power more widely. He regarded his solution as a moderate one (5):

I gave the common people as much privilege as is sufficient for them . . . and I contrived that those who had power and were admired for their prosperity should themselves suffer nothing *aeikes* (unseemly).

[1] See p. 143 for the political advantages to be derived from success at the games in fifth-century Athens.

Our concern here is with the manner in which Solon understood the problem and its solution, and the terms in which he evaluated it. He held (4, 1 ff.) that Athens would never be destroyed by Zeus or the other immortal gods, since the Athenians had Pallas Athena as their protectress goddess; and she would protect them from patriotic motives. No; the citizens themselves and their leaders will bring the city to disaster, if disaster there is to be (4, 5 ff.):

> The citizens themselves by their folly are willing to destroy this mighty city, persuaded by (or 'obeying') wealth; and the mind of the leaders of the people is *adikos* (unjust), and they are about to suffer many woes as a result of great *hubris*; for they do not know how to restrain excess. . . . They grow wealthy, persuaded by unjust deeds . . . and without respect for sacred or public property they steal, one from one source, one from another, and do not heed the august foundations of Justice, who in silence knows what is and what has been, and in due time comes to punish.

Solon next prophesies civil war, slavery and all manner of general civic calamity. Then (4, 27 ff.):

> Thus a public *kakon* (disaster) comes to the *oikos* of each individual, and the courtyard gates are no longer able to keep it out: it jumps over the high hedge and finds every man, even if he flees to the deepest recesses of his chamber. These things my heart bids me tell the Athenians, that *dusnomiā* (the opposite of *eunomia*) causes very many *kaka* (disasters) to the city, whereas *eunomia* makes all things orderly and appropriate, and often puts fetters on the *adikoi* (unjust); while *eunomia* makes the rough smooth, checks excess, brings *hubris* to obscurity, and withers the blossoming flowers of *ate* (destruction), makes straight crooked judgments, soothes proud deeds, ends the works of civic discord and calms the anger of grievous strife; and all things as a result of *eunomia* are appropriate and fitting in the world of men.

This analysis is very 'naturalistic' for its period. The opening lines of the poem, which exclude the Olympians as causes

48

of any disaster to Athens, give an opportunity for an explanation in human terms; and Solon shows considerable understanding of what is happening. The point, however, must not be overstated. Justice is spoken of in personal terms, and it seems difficult to exclude an element of personification from *eunomia* and *dusnomia* when used as they are used in 27 ff. At this period personification or deification of what we should regard as an abstraction or a concrete entity does not exclude other modes of thinking of it, even in circumstances which must appear startling to us. In 36, 3 ff. Solon says

> There is one who would bear excellent witness in the court of Time—the great mother of the Olympian gods, dark Earth, whose landmarks planted everywhere I once removed, so that she who was once a slave is now free.

Solon evidently finds no difficulty in the 'transition', in consecutive lines, from Earth, a divine person, mother of the Olympians, to earth, dark earth, in which boundary markers may be planted. For him there is indeed no transition: the two ideas co-exist with no feeling of contradiction. This state of mind, so difficult for us to imagine, is characteristic at this period even of a Solon: he is an 'advanced' thinker, but an 'advanced' thinker of the sixth century. (There is no question here of careless language used when Solon's attention is directed elsewhere: he is attentively thinking and writing of one of the major achievements of his political career.) With this proviso, however, we may say that Solon is feeling his way towards an explanation in terms of 'naturalistic' causes and effects. That his thoughts are expressed in verse does not render them 'poetic' in intention: verse is at this period the form of expression used for anything that is to have as wide a circulation as possible. Solon's intention is to give 'prosaic' political advice.

But what is the situation, and how does Solon analyse it? There appear to be strong resemblances with what was happening elsewhere. Wealth, possessed or desired, is upsetting the old order. Some are becoming richer, some poorer, to an

49

extent that is unfamiliar (28c). Many of the poor have been enslaved, apparently for debt, and sold into other lands (4, 23 ff.). This is not mentioned by other writers we have discussed as happening in their cities; but the evidence for the period as a whole is scanty; and money, in increasing the possibility of borrowing, also increases the possibility of being unable to repay. In Solon's mind, the cause of Athens' woes is that 'the leaders of the people' are becoming wealthy by indiscriminate means, and the citizens, 'persuaded by wealth', are following their leaders in courses which he believes can only bring the city to general disaster. It appears that wealthy individuals, who have benefited from the new economic opportunities, are engaged in faction and competition for political power: there is a possible reference to political clubs or associations (4, 22); and the citizens in general are siding with the faction of one or another powerful and wealthy individual. (The wealth which the citizens 'obey' is, I take it, that of the powerful rich.) The identity of the leaders is unclear. Plutarch (*Life of Solon*, 3) quotes as Solon's the lines which also appear as Theognis 315 ff., 'Many *kakoi* are rich and many *agathoi* poor . . .'; but such passages are not infrequently attributed to more than one author, and the situation seems to suit that of the Theognid corpus better. In a poem (34) quoted by Aristotle in his *Constitution of Athens* (12), whose content confirms its Solonian authorship, Solon says that it did not please him (34, 9 f.)

That the *kakoi* should have *īsomoiriā* (an equal share) of the rich earth with the *agathoi*.

In general, Solon seems little concerned with problems of defining *arete* and the *agathos*. The impression given by the admittedly scanty evidence is not that some previously *kakoi* have become *agathoi*, but that some of the old *agathoi* have become much more wealthy than before; and it is of course no less possible for one of the old *agathoi* to benefit from the new economic opportunities if he will.

Solon wishes to set limits to the activities of these men; and the concept of *eunomia* is a means by which he hopes to attain this end. *Eunomia* was evidently an important political catchword in the sixth century.[1] Its precise meaning has been much discussed; but its effectiveness politically may have lain in its vagueness in ancient Greek. On the basis of its form it is well suited to convey ideas of 'good order', 'good laws' and 'having the laws well obeyed', together with that of an appropriate distribution (*nemesthai*, 'assign') of wealth, power and resources within society. This last idea should be related to the early view[2] of one's *moira*, one's share in life, as setting bounds, social and other, to what one may do or expect to experience. In a static, traditional society the actual 'shares' are held to be the right ones: one's *moira* is not only one's share but one's due share. Such an attitude would make it easy to use *eunomia*, 'the appropriate distribution', as a conservative term, and there are indications of such overtones; but the word denotes no precise state of affairs, and in a period of social, political and economic upheaval might well be widely attractive, and useful to one who, like Solon, was aiming at a consensus and a moderate solution: who could be against 'good order' and 'an appropriate distribution of resources within society'? (To say this is not to say that Solon had not a precise idea of what he himself held to be a condition in which *eunomia* was present.) The benefits that Solon promises as the fruit of *eunomia* would certainly be widely desired, and difficult to obtain in the sixth century.

Since *eunomia* is so vague, and its implications may vary from one writer to another, we must now try to establish Solon's interpretation of it. He regards himself as a moderate (6):

> The common people would follow its leaders best if it were neither too little restrained nor yet subject to compulsion by force; for surfeit breeds *hubris* when much *olbos* (prosperity) comes to those whose state of mind is not appropriate.

[1] One of Tyrtaeus' poems is said to have been entitled *eunomia* (Strabo 8, 362,) and Xenophanes 2, 19 (see p. 47) promises it as the effect of his *sophia*.

[2] Above, p. 19 f., below, pp. 87 ff.; and see also *Merit and Responsibility* pp. 17 ff.

(The nature of the *hubris* of the common people will be discussed in the next chapter.[1]) This when combined with 34, 9 ff., quoted above, seems to indicate that he wished to remove economic injustice and hardship—and, as his political reforms make clear, widen the basis of political power and participation—without radically affecting the structure of society: *agathoi* and *kakoi* should remain in their appointed place.

More of Solon's position becomes clear from poem 13. He prays to the Muses (3 ff.):

> Grant me *olbos* (prosperity) from the blessed gods, and that I always am accorded good reputation by men. And may I be sweet to my *philoi* (friends) and bitter to my *echthroi* (enemies), revered by the one and feared by the other. I desire to possess wealth, but not to possess it unjustly; just punishment always comes afterwards; the wealth that the gods give remains with a man permanently . . . whereas the wealth that men pursue by *hubris* does not come in an orderly decent manner, but against its will, persuaded by unjust deeds; and swiftly disaster is mingled with it. . . .

The beginnings of disaster are small, but soon grow; and Zeus strikes suddenly in punishment. He is not always quick to anger, but he punishes in the end. Solon (29 ff.) expresses the same belief as Theognis about the punishment of children for the wrongdoing of parents, but without Theognis' complaint that such punishment is unjust. There follows (41 ff.) an account of different ways in which men strive to rise from poverty to wealth, to which is added (63 ff.) the general reflection:

> It is *moira* that brings *kakon* and *esthlon* upon mortals, and the gifts of the immortal gods cannot be escaped. There is danger in all actions, and no-one knows at the beginning of a matter how it will end. No; he who tries to act *eu* (successfully, effectively) falls unawares into some great and dire disaster, while to him that acts *kakōs* (ineffectively) the god furnishes good fortune as his deliverance from folly. There

[1] See below, pp. 87 ff.

is no clear limit for wealth established among mankind; for those who now have the greatest riches among us strive to double them. Who could satisfy them all? *The immortals furnish gains for mortal men.* But *ate* (disaster) comes from them, disaster which attends now upon one man, now upon another, when Zeus sends it to *tinesthai.*

The second part of this passage resembles Theognis 227 ff.,[1] with some significant exceptions. The Theognid poet has 'possessions turn to folly for mortal men' in place of the italicised line which ascribes gains to the agency of the immortals; and for *tinesthai* he has *teiromenois*, 'in their misery'. Why does Solon wish to introduce divine agency into his account of the new limitless pursuit of gain,[2] even though it causes a conflict with the earlier part of his own poem? In 13, 7 ff., he desires god-given wealth, which is permanent; in 13, 74 ff., the immortals furnish gains which bring disaster. A likely reason for the conflict is that Solon has different kinds of gain in mind: we must remember that his society is in a period of rapid transition. What, in fact, is meant by 'god-given wealth' in such passages as Solon 13, 9 and Hesiod *Works and Days* 320? The contrast in Hesiod is with wealth gained by force or through the agency of a deceitful tongue; in Solon with wealth gained by injustice or *hubris*. If we consider an agricultural society such as that of Homer, where there is no money, wealth is in the hands of the landowners, who have only two methods of increasing their prosperity: by natural increase of crops and herds, and by raiding for booty; and it might well be empirically true, as well as a useful belief, that booty was likely to be quickly lost in a counter-raid. So far as it persisted, such raiding together with theft and the doubtfully legal manner in which Perses apparently acquired his inheritance will continue to serve for 'wealth got by violence'. But the invention of money makes possible new methods of becoming rich, methods which are to be sharply

[1] For the first part, cf. Theognis 133 ff. For 227 ff., see above, p. 38.

[2] Aristotle, *Politics* 1256b30 ff., supposes Solon to be approving of the limitless pursuit of gain, and criticises him in the light of general Aristotelian philosophy.

distinguished from theft and piracy, but which also have little resemblance to the method of increase of field and flock. For Hesiod, all lawful (but non-litigious) methods of becoming more prosperous by one's own efforts are aspects of 'good strife'; for Theognis, the new methods, which enable the *kakoi* to become prosperous, are detestable, so that though, like all early Greeks, he piously ascribes success and failure to the gods (as in 133 ff.), he does not mention the gods here where he is directly referring to the new economic situation. Solon does not reject the new methods, though he wishes to impose limits; but the opening lines of poem 13 seem to reflect the traditional view of the agriculturalist. From 41 ff., however, he turns to the means by which the poor man may rise from his poverty; and this directs his thoughts to the complexities of economic life in Athens as he knows it. Then (63 ff.) he makes a transition to those who have prospered greatly in the new situation, acknowledges that their gains are god-given, but insists that such gains are precarious; as in the early stages of a new economic system might well be the case. To bring this about, Zeus *tinesthai*—not necessarily 'punishes', but 'deprives of *time*';[1] there seems no suggestion at all here that such gains are of their nature wrongful or unjust. On the contrary, by emphasising that they are god-given Solon is fitting them into his world-picture, and into the world-picture of the Athenians for whom he is writing, as 'part of the nature of things', and creating a new, or rather extended, frame of reference for the new situation. There is a conflict in the poem, for within its seventy-six lines occurs the enlargement of the poet's world-view.

Solon acknowledged the acceptability of the new means of making money; but he evidently wished to set limits: in a situation that was doubtless different from Hesiod's, he had not Hesiod's cheerful confidence in the essential innocence of maximising one's wealth by all forms of 'good strife': he had seen the social consequences in Attica. Nevertheless, prosperity, *olbos*, is his goal, and that of the society around him. Having benefited the poor and restored many who had even been enslaved abroad, he must have been assured of a following

[1] See Chapter II, p. 14 f.

with whose aid he could have made himself a tyrant. He did not; and he is aware of the manner in which his refusal is to be evaluated. Poem 32 runs thus:

> If I have spared my native land, and did not put my hand to tyranny and harsh violence, having befouled and *kataischunein* my good name, I am not *aideisthai* (ashamed); for thus I think I shall the more *nīkān* (surpass, triumph over) all mankind.

Again, poem 33 imagines a comment of what Plutarch, who preserves the fragment, terms the *polloi kai phauloi*, the lower classes:[1]

> Solon, it turns out, is no shrewd or clever man; for when the god offered *esthla* (advantages) he himself refused them . . . like one that lacks both spirit and intelligence. Now if I had political power, could gain abundant wealth and rule as tyrant over Athens for a single day, I should be quite willing to be flayed for a wineskin afterwards and have my posterity wiped out.

The standards are quite clear; and they are the standards of *arete*, which enjoin upon the *agathos* that he shall maximise his prosperity and well-being. Solon himself wished to maximise his prosperity and well-being; but evidently believed that injustice and lack of moderation would be punished either in his own person or in his descendants; and he himself was deterred by this. Yet he is aware that his refusal to aim at a tyranny is *aischron* in terms of current Greek values. It is for this reason that he uses *nikan* of his conduct, to render it by implication *kalon*, since victory is *kalon*; but poem 33 shows the power of the values that he is resisting. For Solon too, *arete*, the goal of life, is evaluated in terms of prosperity and good reputation; and for him too the primary loyalty is to a group smaller than the city: 'may I be sweet to my *philoi* and bitter to my *echthroi*' (13, 5). An active politician's *philoi* are his political supporters, his *echthroi*, his political opponents; and history shows the lengths to which Greek politicians were prepared to go in order to help their *philoi* and harm their

[1] For the views of *agathoi* on tyranny, see below, pp. 68 ff.

55

echthroi. Solon, holding such values, was doubtless partly restrained by fear of divine retribution, partly by his view of the
effects of *eunomia* and *dusnomia.* When thinking in terms of
eunomia and *dusnomia,* he concerns himself with their effects first
on the city as a whole, then on the household of the individual;
and despite his view of the appropriate behaviour towards
philoi and *echthroi,* he is evidently also capable of thinking in
terms of the well-being of the city as a whole. The manner in
which his argument is expressed, however, shows that he is
aware that his audience are concerned primarily with their
own households, and must be shown that they cannot escape
the consequences of general *dusnomia.* Solon may have been
restrained by such considerations; but the *arete*-values of his
society, which he does not definitively reject—he does not say
'it is not *aischron* to decline a tyranny which one might obtain'
—and indeed except where tyranny is in question accepts,
give no means of effectively restraining anyone who was prepared to chance what the gods might do, and felt himself
sufficiently powerful to aim, with his supporters, at a tyranny.
Far from restraining, such *arete*-values enjoin upon the individual *agathos* that he shall secure himself a tyranny if he can.
(The attitude of his fellow-citizens will be discussed below.)[1]
As a restraint, the idea of *eunomia* has the disadvantages that to
contravene its requirements, for example by becoming a
tyrant, is evidently not *aischron,* so that where *eunomia* conflicts
with *arete, arete* is stronger; that it denotes no very clear state
of affairs; and that even if a would-be tyrant agreed with
Solon that the general ills of *dusnomia* affect the individual
household, he might well suppose that he could ensure that
those who were adversely affected were his *echthroi,* his political
opponents, while his *philoi* prospered. Solon was a major
political thinker of the sixth century, and his solutions are the
fruit of much thought; but it was not only the economic
situation and the political institutions of Solon's Athens that
required attention, but its most powerfully held values, which
remained, and were long to remain, disruptive, since they
encouraged civil strife in the interests of one's own faction. In
the light of the situation as a whole, it is not surprising that

[1] Pp. 68 ff.

56

Solon's solution failed, and the rule of the Pisistratids soon followed: indeed, Athens was fortunate in that her tyrants showed such moderation.[1]

In Hesiod, Theognis and Solon, accordingly, we see three responses to the new social and economic situations that resulted from the introduction of a money-economy. (Tyrtaeus' poems are a response to the very special situation of Sparta, and are linked with the establishment of the unique Spartan state: at the level of its *agathoi*, an armed camp; and economically, a state as detached from the money-economy of the rest of Greece as possible.) Hesiod and Solon were both perceptive men but, not surprisingly, were prevented by the complexity of the problem from producing a solution likely to secure the prosperity and stability they desired. Though the poems of the Theognid corpus were produced in a partisan spirit, the very circumstances of their production directed their authors' attention to the values of society. One striking insight was attained; but the following chapter will show that we have no evidence that the insight persisted.

[1] In Greek, a 'tyrant' is a ruler who has gained power through unconstitutional means, He need not behave in a manner which we should characterize as 'tyrannical,' though many Greek tyrants were tyrants in both senses.

4

The Earlier Fifth Century

A. Introductory

When studying history, we should always remember that centuries are artificial units of time; and when studying ancient history, we should always remember that what we term the centuries B.C. are artificial units of which the ancient world was unaware. If a society uses a certain measure of time and accords significance to some of its units, then the fact that it supposes itself to be passing from one significant unit to another may produce observable phenomena, whether the unit be a *saeculum*, a century, a decade or the Age of Aquarius; but the Greeks, of course, did not suppose that a new major period of time was beginning in the year which we term 500 B.C.

However, an event of major importance to the Greeks occurred in the early years of the fifth century: the Persian Wars. As a result of their experiences in these wars, the Greeks changed their outlook and attitudes both to each other and to those who were not Greeks, and began to set themselves apart as 'Hellenes' from '*barbaroi*', the inferior peoples who inhabited the rest of the world. The elegies of Simonides which were composed for those Greeks who fell in the fighting sound a note that is not heard before the Persian Wars, as in 127:

> If the greatest part of *arete* is to die *kalōs*, fortune has granted this to us above all men; for we lie here and enjoy a glory that does not grow old, since we strove to set a crown of freedom upon Greece.

Arete commends the traditional qualities here: it is the idea that its purpose is to defend the freedom of Greece as a whole that is new. The dangers of subjugation by an external enemy produced the feeling of unity expressed here. The history of the Persian Wars indicates that not all Greek cities

58

experienced this feeling during the Wars, and it is likely that all who did experience it experienced it more strongly in retrospect, after the victory; but it served for the future to demarcate 'Hellenes' from '*barbaroi*'.

It did not, however, endow the Greeks with any feeling of unity, or any powerful desire to co-operate, once the external threat had been removed. The freedom and autonomy of the individual city-state remained their ideal, even though it was an ideal encroached upon by Athens as the century developed. No city-state was very large; some were very small; and all had to defend themselves against possible or actual attacks from their neighbours. The Persian Wars liberated new energies, particularly among the Athenians; but the basic situation in which the Greek lived—or desired to live—remained the same.

In turning to our evidence for the earlier fifth century, we shall be concerned chiefly with the lyric poets Pindar and Bacchylides, the tragedians Aeschylus and Sophocles, and the historian Herodotus. Since the purpose of these writers is not didactic or hortatory in the manner of those considered in the last chapter, it will be convenient to discuss the earlier fifth century in terms of theme rather than to treat each author separately. Sophocles and Herodotus both exemplify traditional values, which indeed continued to exist long after the period discussed here, and also show signs of new developments which will be the subject of the next chapter. The extant works of both all belong to the second half of the fifth century, but their basic attitudes were formed in the first half;[1] and it is in any case with types of attitude and belief, not with the *precise* date of their expression by a particular writer, that we are concerned here. All these writers are, as is to be expected, *agathoi*; but of Pindar and Bacchylides more must be said. They were writing victory-odes for successful contestants in the great games of Greece; and to be a contestant already required financial resources. True, most events were much less expensive than chariot-racing, to which only the wealthiest could aspire;[2] but to compete even in a

[1] Sophocles was born *c.* 496, Herodotus *c.* 485.
[2] See pp. 142 ff. for Alcibiades.

foot-race required leisure and a trainer; and if a victory, once won, were to be celebrated in song, only the wealthy could afford to be patrons of such poets as Pindar and Bacchylides. The victors celebrated in their poems are a sub-class within the class of the *agathoi*; and it will be of interest to observe how they evaluate their own position, their relationship to the other members of society, and the likely attitude of other members of society to them.

How then do these authors, who constitute the bulk of our evidence for the values of the earlier fifth century, understand and evaluate the questions with which we are concerned?

B. *Agathos* AND *Arete*

The *agathos* traditionally is he who is held to be most effective in assuring the security, stability and well-being of the social unit, in war and in peace. It will be convenient to examine the use of *agathos* and *arete* in the earlier fifth century separately in war and in peace. The purpose is merely to make the exposition clearer: the words of course commend a complete view of life.

In war, the *agathos* is still the effective fighter; and it remains *kalon* to succeed, *aischron* to fail. So in Aeschylus (*Persians* 331 f.) Atossa, on learning of the Persian disasters, laments:

Ah woe, these are the greatest of *kaka* (disasters) . . . an occasion for shrill lamentation and *aischos*.

Defeat is *aischron* even when the gods cause it. When the Argive army was routed in its attack on Thebes (Pindar, *Nemeans* IX, 24 ff.):

Zeus with his all-powerful thunderbolt split the deep-breasted earth for Amphiaraus, and hid him in it with his horses and chariot, before his warrior spirit could suffer what was *aischron* by his being struck in the back by the spear of Periclymenus. When panic is sent from heaven even the children of the gods turn to flight.

Had Amphiaraus been present in the army when the gods sent a panic upon it, so that he fled and was defeated and killed with the rest, this would have been *aischron* for him. There is

60

no acceptable excuse for panic and defeat, even in the narration of a myth where the rôle of the gods is known as it cannot be known in real life. The successful defence of the city-state is so important that the demand for success in battle is absolute and unqualified. The demand extends to success in attacking another state: Amphiaraus is in the attacking force here; and here, though we may say that failure in attack may lead to the defeat of one's city in a counter-attack, and though the loss of one's army, or any considerable part of it, renders such a counter-attack the more easy, doubtless shame at defeat as such has its part to play. This is both a results-culture, whose values are deeply influenced by the absolute demand that certain goals be successfully attained, and a shame-culture, whose sanction, in addition to the disastrous nature of certain failures in themselves, is *overtly* 'what people will say'. Sometimes, as in failure to win in the games, there is little material loss; but failure is *aischron* nonetheless, and will be mocked, by one's *echthroi* at all events. Nevertheless, the results-culture is more basic: it is the need for success in maintaining the prosperity and stability of the city-state that most powerfully influences the nature of *arete* and the *agathos*, and consequently what is held to be *aischron*. For not only must the city-state be defended, it must be defended at once and in a particular manner. Herodotus puts into the mouth of the Persian general Mardonius (VII, 9) the comment that the Greeks fight in the most foolish manner, since they choose the most level ground. Herodotus is either hinting at the ignorance of Mardonius, or being disingenuous. The defending army had to meet the invaders on the level land, the corn-land, and at once: they could not lurk in the hills and await the best opportunity; for if they did, and the enemy burnt the crops, the defenders might well starve before the next harvest. Brasidas in Thucydides (IV, 87) reminds the Acanthians of this; and, though secure behind their walls, they came over to his side 'out of fear for the crops' (88).

This being the case, those who are held to be most effective fighters on such level ground,[1] the heavy-armed infantry, the

[1] Cavalry too were *agathoi*, but scarce; and the Greeks had not at this period discovered the effectiveness of missile attacks made

hoplites, will evidently be held to contribute most to the well-being and indeed the continued existence of the city; so that it is not surprising to find them commended as *agathoi*. In such commendation of the hoplites a social class is commended. Citizens must buy their own armour; hoplite armour is expensive; so that only comparatively wealthy citizens can be effective in war, and so *agathoi*. To be brave, to have a strong right arm, is of little use in such infantry warfare if one has no armour. (The rôle of Athens' navy will be discussed in the next chapter.)

On the other hand, though wealth is necessary, it is not sufficient; and here we may begin to consider the range of *agathos* and *arete* in peacetime. Bacchylides (29, 159 ff.) writes:

> I say and ever shall that *arete* has the highest glory. Wealth consorts also with *deiloi*, though it does exalt a man's thoughts; and he who benefits the gods gladdens his heart with a more glorious hope; and if, mortal though he be, he enjoys good health and can live on what he possesses, he vies with the greatest. There is delight to be had in every human life that is free from disease and *amēchanos* (helpless) poverty. The desire of the wealthy for great things and the desire of him who has less for lesser things are equal. To have a sufficiency of all things gives no pleasure to mortals. No; they ever seek to catch what eludes them. He whose heart is disturbed by trivial anxieties acquires *time* only during his lifetime. *Arete* demands toil, but when completed aright it leaves a man even when he is dead an enviable monument of fame.

Evidently the recipient of this ode, one Argeius of Ceos, victor in the boys' boxing-match at the Isthmus, does not belong to the wealthiest families of Ceos; and evidently not all of the latter have *arete* as Bacchylides understands the word.

---

by light-armed and so highly mobile troops against hoplites who moved much more slowly and had no missile weapons. Demosthenes learned the lesson in Aetolia and with Cleon applied it against the Spartans at Sphacteria (Thucydides III, 97 f. and IV, 28, 4 ff.)

It is equally evident that Argeius' family is not poor: almost all Greeks in the heyday of the city-state agreed that poverty cripples *arete*; as it must, if *arete* is interpreted as the needs of the city-state seemed to require. For Bacchylides, *arete* commends the hard training leading to fitness and success in the games—and in war, if need be—engaged in by those whose financial position affords them the necessary leisure and equipment. In Ceos, they are, it seems, neither the only wealthy, nor the most wealthy, citizens. Those who give themselves over to 'trivial anxieties' and gain *time* (which here seems to commend both status and the material prosperity on which it is based, as in Homer), but only during their own lifetime, are presumably the wealthy *deiloi* of the earlier lines quoted; and these must surely be merchants, whose anxieties gain them *time*, but whose concerns are trivial in Bacchylides' eyes. Bacchylides is endeavouring to deny status to such men, and he does indeed term them *deiloi*;[1] but he cannot deny their *time*, though he denies them fame after death; and he acknowledges that if they 'benefit the gods' by offering them sacrifices, they can hope for the benefits of heaven in return: a question to be discussed further below. Indeed, elsewhere Bacchylides has to concede a higher, though still secondary, status to wealth in itself (37, 47 ff.):

> The most *kalon* state of affairs is for an *esthlos* to be admired by many; but I know also the power of great wealth, which renders even the useless man *chrēstos* (useful).

The *esthlos*, the man of adequate wealth who undertakes the approved rôles in war and in peace, is most admirable; but even if he does not take part in games as an *esthlos* should—in Athens, at all events, he would have to serve as a hoplite—the man of mere money makes a contribution that must be acknowledged, and highly: Bacchylides treats the possession of wealth as less *kalon*, but its possessor is useful, *chrestos*; and *chrestos* used absolutely of persons is a virtual synonym of *agathos* and *esthlos*, and has similar commendatory power.

[1] Presumably for some reason they did not serve as hoplites, possibly because their 'trivial anxieties' entailed much travelling; cf. Theognis' Megara, p. 40 above.

The contribution of money in itself to the stability and well-being of the Greek city-state is being recognised. The effects of this on Athenian life will be discussed in the next chapter.

Agathos and *arete*, then, commend the activities in war and in peace of those who are held to make most contribution to the prosperity and stability of the state, together with other activities which also require money and leisure, and which, being not available, or less available, to other members of society, consequently enjoy high prestige. Membership of this favoured group will vary from city to city in accordance with its history and constitution. Where, as in Theognis' Megara, there are many new recruits to the ranks of the privileged, 'high birth'—membership of a family which has owned considerable property, preferably land, for some generations— may, after a struggle, cease to be important, since the contribution of money to the well-being of the city is now acknowledged.[1] Elsewhere, the old landowners may continue to be the most wealthy, to make the most contribution to the city, to enjoy the highest prestige, and to be credited with political skill. So Pindar includes in his praise of a Pythian victor (X, 69 ff.):

> We shall praise his *esthloi* brothers, in that they increase the state of Thessaly and cause it to flourish; it is in the hands of *agathoi* that resides the good piloting of cities, inherited from father to son.

Pindar, in writing for a Thessalian aristocrat, is unlikely to deny the heritability of political skill; and at a time when all such skill is 'rule of thumb' passed on within families, such *agathoi* families, being those who had actually wielded power, were the repositories of all the political skill that existed. Furthermore, it must never be forgotten that Greek values provide the strongest inducement to deference by the *kakoi* to

[1] In time, of course, the new *agathoi* may become as exclusive as the old. The *agathoi* families of later fifth century Athens must have included some whose ancestors would not have been so considered a century earlier; but our *agathoi* sources are little disposed to regard Cleon (below, pp. 65, 140 f.) as an *agathos*, though he had claims to be so regarded.

the *agathoi*. To be an *agathos* is to be a good specimen of human being, to be a human being at his best; to be a *kakos* is to be the reverse. It would be very difficult for one termed *kakos*, who could not fail to observe the contribution to the well-being of the city made by the *agathos* in virtue of his wealth, to deny that he himself was of less value, was an inferior specimen of human being; and how could he then claim to be more fitted to rule, or to take part in any other admired activity, than the *agathos*? Even when a state enjoys a democratic constitution, the *kakoi* are likely to be deterred from speaking in the assembly, and unlikely to be elected to office, though they can of course vote. In fifth-century Athens not merely wealthy citizens but members of aristocratic families continue to be elected to the highest offices long after the democratisation of Athens' institutions; and when a Cleon comes to the fore our sources write of him as though he were a poor journeyman tanner rather than the prosperous owner of a tannery with abundant money and leisure to devote to politics. Money or no, democratic Athens seems—or our *agathoi* authors seem—reluctant to acknowledge that he is an *agathos*, or could possibly have any political skill. There is, accordingly, some difficulty, even in a Greek democracy, for wealth unaccompanied by 'good family' to be acknowledged as *arete*, at all events where that *arete* is to be translated into political influence.[1]

The position in which a *kakos*, someone deficient in money, birth, prowess and status, might find himself *vis-à-vis* an *agathos* who possessed the valued characteristics is shown clearly by the portrayal of Teucer's difficulties when faced with Menelaus and the other *agathoi* in Sophocles' *Ajax*. Even if Sophocles' purpose is in part to argue that Teucer's disabilities are the result of mere prejudice on the part of the *agathoi*, the portrayal on the stage indicates the likely response of the *agathos* in real life. Teucer is the son of Telamon, a Greek *agathos*, and a foreign queen captured and given to Telamon as part of his booty in war; he is not, as Ajax was, a legitimate son of

[1] It seems to be very important to Thucydides (IV, 27 ff.) to deny the possibility that Cleon's success at Sphacteria could have resulted from military skill, which would have increased his claim to be an *agathos*.

65

Telamon, and is armed as an archer, a (socially) inferior weapon. Teucer has been resisting Menelaus' attempts to deny due rites to the dead Ajax; and the following altercation occurs (1120 ff.):

MENELAUS: The archer appears to have no small opinion of himself.

TEUCER: I have; for not 'banausic' is the (archer's) art that I possess.

MENELAUS: You would utter loud boasts if you were to get possession of a shield (and become a hoplite).

TEUCER: Even light-armed I should be a match for you in hoplite armour.

MENELAUS: How terribly does your tongue nourish your spirit!

TEUCER: One may 'think big' when justice is on one's side.

If the last line is taken in isolation, it appears that to have justice on one's side gives one a claim that the *arete* of the *agathos* cannot override; but Teucer has in the earlier lines argued that his *technē*, art, craft, skill, is not 'banausic'—as are the *technai* of artisans—and that Menelaus is such a poor fighter that he could defeat him even though he is himself not a hoplite. (The fact that, on rough terrain favourable to them, light-armed troops can regularly defeat hoplites, was not yet known to the Greeks. When discovered, it caused great confusion to the traditional *agathoi*, the hoplites.) Furthermore, elsewhere Teucer emphasises that not only was his father an outstanding warrior, but that his mother was a queen in her own country (1299 ff.). The most that Sophocles seems able to assert—and doubtless all that he wished to assert, for he was in most matters a far from radical thinker—is that if one is a good and brave fighter, not engaged in 'banausic' *techne*, then, even if one is not a hoplite, the sense of the justice of one's case may give one confidence even to answer back to an *agathos*. Were one engaged in a 'banausic' *techne*, or an ineffective warrior, one might well have difficulty in obtaining one's rights; and even Teucer regards his behaviour as 'thinking big', *mega phronein*, a phrase which we should sometimes render

66

'being haughty', not as a mere expression of undoubted rights. The habitual deference of the *kakos* is reflected in the scene, and also in Teucer's words (1093 ff.):

> I should no longer be surprised at a man who was a 'mere nothing' in respect of birth *hamartanein* (erring) when those who seem to be *eugeneis* (of good birth) produce such erring judgments in their speeches.

Teucer has been startled out of his deference, his assumption that the well-born, the *agathoi*, have sound judgment in all matters. Sophocles wishes the audience to take note; as well he might, for, as we have seen, the inducements to thoughtless deference to the *agathos* are very powerful. (We shall discover that the advantages of the *agathos* persist even in the law-courts of democratic Athens in the later fifth and fourth centuries.)

The *kakos*, then, has great difficulty in maintaining his claims to just treatment against the *agathos*. It would be difficult to enumerate any 'undoubted rights' that he possesses. Certainly he possesses none merely in virtue of his being human; what rights he has, he has in virtue of his membership of a particular group; and if the group to which he belongs accords few effective rights to the *kakos*, he has few effective rights. In Athens, the state made certain forms of financial relief available to poor citizens, which increased in size and number as the fifth century progressed; but his redress in law, should he be wronged by an *agathos*, was, as we shall see, much more difficult to secure than might be expected in what was in name a democracy governed by law, according, it was claimed, equal rights before that law to all of its citizens.

Accordingly, the *agathos* may well feel drawn to strive to the limit for success, in the early fifth century as in earlier periods; for *arete* appears to be just as competitive as it was in Homer and the writers discussed in the last chapter. The more success, the more *arete*; and the person who has the most *arete* of all, in a city that contains one, is the tyrant, the tyrant who was the recipient of so many, though by no means all, of the odes of Simonides, Pindar and Bacchylides; for *arete* is manifested first and foremost in one's prosperity and that of one's

67

oikos and *philoi*, 'friends', and in the qualities which serve to produce or maintain that prosperity; and who more than the tyrant has fulfilled the requirements of *arete*?

It may appear strange that the tyrant should fulfil the highest ideals of a society supposedly dedicated to the idea of *eleutheriā*, translated 'freedom'. However, 'freedom' or 'liberty' is a concept which cannot readily be translated from one culture to another. Our own usage of the English words is complex. In the minds of some, 'liberty' is characteristically associated with such ideas as equality and fraternity, when it should commend the co-operative association of free and equal persons. For others, 'freedom'—'freedom' rather than 'liberty', for the semantic behaviour of the words is different—denotes and commends the ability and the right of the individual to behave as he will. Subject, of course, to the requirements of law, we should add; but the requirements of law differ widely in different societies; and this notion of 'freedom' is at all events basically competitive, and lays emphasis on the rights of the individual, rather than those of society. Greek *eleutheria* is an extreme form of the competitive concept of freedom; and we shall see the difficulties experienced in attempting to subject the *eleutheros* to the rule of law, even in the law-courts of democratic Athens. Furthermore, the unit of society which, as we shall see more clearly in the next chapter, commands the most powerful loyalties remains the individual household, with its *philoi*. To advance the success and *eleutheria* of one's own *oikos* and *philoi* at the expense of the rest is an enterprise which will be vigorously opposed by other citizens who regard themselves as *agathoi*; but it cannot be effectively condemned in *arete*-terms, for it is the maximising of such success and *eleutheria* that is the mark of *arete*. The tyrant has become most *agathos* and most *eleutheros*, for *eleutheria* is manifested in ruling over others and in not submitting to the rule of others oneself.

In Greece, a tyrant is one who arrives at supreme power by unconstitutional means: the word does not necessarily imply that, having secured supreme power, the tyrant behaves 'tyrannically', that is, cruelly. Herodotus (I, 59) records that Pisistratus did not rule in an arbitrary manner, but with moderation and efficiency. Yet he had gained power un-constitutionally, and his rule is termed a tyranny (I, 60). The tyrants seem frequently to have risen to power by championing the cause of the *kakoi*; who, as we have seen, may well have felt the need of a powerful champion, and so supported him. The *agathoi*, on the other hand, were certain to be hostile and resentful: by outstripping them in success and prosperity, and also by reducing their *eleutheria*, inasmuch as he himself was set above them and protected the *kakoi*, who were below them, he was reducing their *arete* and placing them in a situation that was *aischron*. The *kakoi* are unlikely to have felt envy or resentment: inferior specimens of human beings as they were, *qua kakoi*, and deferential to the *agathoi* above them, they had no *arete* to be smirched by submission, and were likely to recognise the tyrant's presence as a benefit to themselves. Our sources are all *agathoi*, and naturally not well-disposed in general to tyrants. Tyrants were, however, the patrons of lyric poets; and patrons can expect praise. Pindar praises Hiero of Syracuse (*Pythians* III, 70 f.) for being

> Gentle to the citizens, not jealous of the *agathoi*, and an 'admired father' to strangers.

The contrast with Herodotus III, 80 will bring out the full force of this praise. The latter passage is heavily tinctured with 'sophistic' thought; but it will nevertheless serve to show the manner in which tyranny was evaluated. Otanes thus criticises monarchy, the 'rule of one'. (The reference is immediately to the Persian king, but he is speaking in general terms, and uses 'tyranny' of the situation):

> The enjoyment of supreme power would cause even the most *agathos* of all men . . . to abandon his customary modes of thought; for *hubris* is engendered in him by his present *agatha* (good fortune) and *phthonos* (envy) dwells in men by nature from the beginning; and since he feels both *hubris* and *phthonos*, he has all *kakotes*; for he commits many wicked deeds, some from *hubris*, some from *phthonos*. A tyrant ought to be without *phthonos*, for he has all the *agatha*; but his attitude to the citizens is quite the opposite: he feels *phthonos*

69

for the most *agathoi* while they live and survive, and takes delight in the most *kakoi* of the citizens.[1]

Agathos in the first line of this quotation, and *kakotes*, are affected by the later thought of the century, for they commend the presence, and decry the absence, of co-operative excellences; but the rest of the passage is 'traditional'. The tyrant is filled with *hubris* by his success. One might have expected that others would feel *phthonos*, while their envy would produce in the tyrant suspicion of their likely plots against him. But we must remember that the *agathoi* are giving this account of the tyrant's attitudes; and they are flattered by attributing his behaviour to envy of them. (Should he be a successful commercial 'upstart', as some tyrants were, they could well console themselves by denying him to be an *agathos*, and by supposing him to agree, so that envy might appear an appropriate response.)

In fact, whether or no the tyrant feels *phthonos* for the *agathoi*, the *agathoi* will feel *phthonos* for him; for their *arete* is competitive, and he has outstripped them in political success, *eleutheria* to do what he wishes and general well-being. The attitude of an *agathos* to a more successful *agathos* is shown in a later passage of the same discussion, in which Darius is championing monarchy against oligarchy (III, 82):

> In an oligarchy, when many people are practising *arete* in politics, powerful private hatreds are wont to arise; for, inasmuch as each wishes to be leader and to have his views *nikan* (prevail) they come to have powerful hatreds for each other, as a result of which *stasis* (civil strife) develops, and as a result of civil strife, bloodshed, and as a result of bloodshed the rule of one man.

Competitive *arete* enjoins civil strife on anyone who suffers political defeat, for such defeat is *aischron*, and shows one to be inferior, *kakos*. To remove such a stain any means are justified: the values of Greece, inadequately 'civic', *enjoin* civil strife

[1] Note the manner in which Plato (e.g. *Republic* 579E) 'moralises' the notion of the tyrant as one who depends on *kakoi* and *poneroi*; for Plato is decrying most evidently their injustice. But the readiness

70

in certain, by no means uncommon, circumstances on the *agathos*. When the tyrant has become supremely successful and so supremely *agathos*, all the other *agathoi* are in an *aischron* condition: he might well be suspicious and fearful.[1]

Those who needed protection or help, however, might well welcome one who could offer it, even if he secured supreme power as a result. The would-be tyrant might well appeal to the less privileged citizens, the *kakoi*, as one who would secure justice for them. Herodotus says of the Mede Deioces that (I, 96) 'smitten with desire for a tyranny, he acted as follows'. He lived at a time when the Medes lived in scattered villages, and there was much lawlessness in the land. He made himself well known for his justice in his own village, with the result that his fellow-villagers made him their judge; 'and he, inasmuch as he was aiming at supreme power, was fair and just'. The inhabitants of the surrounding villages heard of this, and, having suffered much in the past from unjust decisions, came to Deioces to such an extent that he had no leisure for anything else. He complained that it was to his disadvantage to spend all his time in this manner and neglect his own interests, and declined to serve as a judge any longer. Lawlessness increased, and the friends of Deioces succeeded in persuading the rest that Deioces should be chosen king.

The story need have no detailed resemblance to the career of any Greek tyrant; but the account of Deioces' rise is doubtless from a Greek source and ascribes Greek motives. It should be noted that, as is quite natural in a society where competitive excellences take precedence, Deioces' motive for being a just judge is that he is aiming at supreme power; but his justice need be no less welcome to the weaker citizens for that reason.

If a tyrant, arising at a time of social and economic turmoil and the helplessness and bafflement, *amechania*, that accompanied it, was able to improve the situation, he had a further

---

with which Plato might expect his views to be accepted must have been increased by the traditional view of the *agathoi* that the tyrant relied on the support of those who were socially *kakoi*, an overtone still possessed by *kakos* in Plato's own usage.

[1] I shall discuss in the next chapter, pp. 145 ff., the difficult position of *agathoi* in extreme democracies.

reason for claiming to be *agathos*. A tyrant has cured *amechania*, though of a different kind, in Pindar (*Pythians* II, 19) where, as a result of Hiero's help, Western Locris

After *amechanoi* troubles of war now looks steadfastly.

To be effective and successful, in the military, social or economic spheres, is to be *agathos*.

How, given the range of *arete*, is it possible to ensure that justice is valued by the stronger and obtainable by the weaker? We have seen that the *kakoi* might welcome a tyrant precisely because he could obtain justice for them; and some tyrants seem to have implemented the laws, and doubtless secured justice—or possibly even partisan advantage—for their followers. Once equipped with a bodyguard, however, the tyrant, who had arrived unconstitutionally, might feel strong enough to overset the laws in his own personal interest, to the detriment of *agathoi* and *kakoi* alike. In theory, in a state like Athens, *agathoi* and *kakoi* were equal before the law, the written law publicly displayed, that all might consult. The publication of law represents an advance of great importance; but it should not be overestimated. Other aspects of the administration of law should be taken into account, particularly the amateur nature of Greek jurymen and the complete absence from court of professional lawyers. This can first be studied only in the later fifth century in court, but the pre-eminence of *arete* is continuous and needs to be restrained if justice is to be valued by anyone who desires an end which he believes he can secure by unjust means. What can deter the *agathos* from harming the *kakos* should he so wish; what can induce the juryman to decide not in terms of the *arete*, or lack of *arete*, of a litigant, but in terms of the justice of his case; what can deter an *agathos* from aiming at a tyranny which seems to be within his powers? There will be many instances in all societies in which fear that one will not in fact succeed, but will be punished by one's fellows, or, in the case of the tyrant, be rapidly overthrown if one does succeed, is the effective restraint; but I wish now to discuss what other beliefs, values and attitudes are available in the earlier fifth century as a restraint upon *arete*.

72

C. 'Moral' restraints upon the would-be tyrant

One might be deterred from becoming a tyrant by the dispraise of one's fellows; though since the most powerful values of the society serve to commend competition, effective condemnation will evidently be very difficult. However, since it is the views of the *agathoi* that are reflected in the sources, and each individual *agathos* has the most powerful motives for preventing anyone else from becoming a tyrant, however much he may long to become a tyrant himself, condemnation is likely to be attempted. As a result, in the view of the articulate Greeks, whose recorded opinions are all that we can now ascertain, tyranny is at this period *per se* injustice, *adikiā*. It is unjust to be a tyrant, however one exercises one's tyranny. In Herodotus (V, 92), when the Spartans are proposing to restore the Pisistratid tyranny, Sosicles, a Corinthian, tries to restrain them:

> (Surely mankind will live in the sea and fishes on dry land) when you, Spartans, are destroying states where there is equality of rights in order to bring back tyrannies into the cities, than which nothing is more *adikon* (unjust) nor bloodthirsty. If it seems to you to be *chrēston* (beneficial) that cities should be under the rule of tyrants, do you first set up a tyrant over yourselves . . .

Nothing is more unjust than imposing a tyranny on a state that does not want it; and, not surprisingly, it is not only unjust to impose a tyrant, but to be one, with the corollary that it is just to resign a tyranny one possesses. When the tyranny of Polycrates of Samos fell into his hands, Maeandrius (Herodotus III, 142) wished to be the most *dikaios* of men, but did not succeed. For when he called an assembly and put the proposal that Samos should return to being an *isonomiā* (a state in which there was equality of rights), a Samian called Telesarchus, who was 'a person of note', *dokimos*, among the citizens, said,

> But you at all events are not worthy to rule over us, since you were born *kakos* and are a pest

and demanded that Maeandrius should give an account of the money he had handled; with the result that Maeandrius

73

retained power and imprisoned his political enemies, thinking that one of them would become tyrant if he renounced the office.

Telesarchus was evidently an *agathos*, an upper-class Samian; and regarded Maeandrius as a *kakos*, and so unfit to rule, on grounds of birth. Maeandrius claimed to have disapproved of the rule of Polycrates, who may have been an *agathos*, one of the Samian aristocracy, 'over men similar to himself'—*agathoi*—on the grounds that such rule was unjust. Telesarchus would doubtless have agreed that Polycrates' rule was unjust; and it also placed Telesarchus in an *aischron* situation in acknowledging another *agathos* as his superior. How much worse to be subjected to a *kakos*!

Similarly Cadmus (Herodotus VII, 164)

> On inheriting from his father the tyranny over the inhabitants of Cos, though the tyranny was in a flourishing condition, of his own free will, not out of any fear but from *dikaiosune* (justice) handed over the rule to the inhabitants of Cos and went to Sicily.

The '*isonomia*' proposed for Samos should not necessarily be equated with democracy. Thucydides (III, 62) writes of an 'isonomous' oligarchy, opposed both to *dunasteiā*, here a very close and lawless oligarchy, and to democracy. The word may denote a state in which equality before the law is combined with political power for the few, the *agathoi*. The *kakos* in such a situation probably had serious difficulties in translating into actuality his theoretical equality before the law. We have noticed Teucer's difficulties, admittedly not in a court of law, in a play which presumably reflects the situation in Athens, which, being a democracy, should present the *kakos* with fewer problems in securing his rights; and the next chapter will demonstrate the persisting problems of the *kakos*, and the advantages of the *agathos*, in the democratic courts of democratic Athens in the fifth, and fourth, centuries.

At all events, to become a tyrant is to commit *adikia*, and to be disapproved of by other *agathoi* in one's own city who have not succeeded in obtaining supreme power themselves. *Agathoi*

74

who are not the tyrant's subjects may acknowledge the *adikia* of becoming a tyrant, but express their admiration for those who have successfully committed the supreme *adikia*; as does Thrasymachus in Plato's *Republic* (344B), since such success represents the maximum of *eudaimoniā*, and *eudaimonia* commends and denotes the goal of life, as the next chapter will abundantly demonstrate. Tyranny is *adikia*, but in the words of Iocasta (*Phoenician Women* 549) it is *eudaimōn adikia*; and though Euripides is attempting to disparage tyranny, *eudaimon* commends more powerfully than *adikia* decries. Accordingly, if *adikia* will bring *eudaimonia*—and the tyrant was generally held to be the most *eudaimon*—it may be pursued to the limit by those who have the power. Those who are not his subjects will admire; those *agathoi* who are his subjects will experience envy and hatred, but they cannot even censure him effectively, for he has manifested his *arete*, the most valued quality, to the full. In these circumstances, only the belief that one's prosperity will not be increased by aiming at tyranny, that one will be punished, sooner or later, by men or gods, through overthrow by force or divinely-sent misfortune, can act as an effective deterrent. The extent to which the Greek gods in the fifth century could be relied on to ensure that one could not be unjust and prosper can conveniently be discussed in the next section; for the same gods look down upon those who are already tyrants, those who as yet merely aspire to tyranny, and those who favour the more everyday forms of *adikia*.

D. What deters from injustice?

The tyrant, the aspirant to tyranny, and other unjust individuals, may be restrained by fear of human reprisals, where such seem possible; but we are concerned here to discover what, if any, effective restraints existed to prevent the tyrant, or any other powerful individual, in the earlier fifth century, from pursuing the maximum of advantage by means of the maximum of injustice which he felt able to commit without fear of human reprisals. Praise of other goals might offer a solution; but are there other goals that appear sufficiently attractive?

In *Isthmians* I, 41 ff., an ode for Herodotus of Thebes,[1] Pindar says:

> Whenever anyone with all his energy throws himself into the pursuit of *arete*, with both expense and toil, we should, if we have discovered a magnificent mode of praise, bear him up on it with *gnōmai* (sentiments) that feel no *phthonos*. For it is a light gift for a man of poetical skill to utter a good word in requital for toils of all kinds, and exalt the common glory of (the victor's) country also. For there are different sweet rewards for their efforts for different men, for the shepherd, the ploughman, the fowler and him whom the sea furnishes with livelihood. Every one of *them* strains every effort to defend grievous famine from his belly; but whoever wins fair fame, either in games or in war, receives the highest reward when he is praised, the finest fruit of the tongue of citizens and strangers alike.

For the poor, to gain a livelihood must be their goal: 'seek a livelihood, and *arete* when a livelihood is attained'. The *agathos*, however, says Pindar, strives, whether in the games or in war, for no material gain for himself, and expects praise as his reward; and he deserves praise, for his victories, whether in war or in the games, redound to the common *kalon*, glory of the city.[2]

Xenocrates of Acragas, brother of the tyrant Theron, is praised as follows (*Isthmians* II, 35 ff.):

> May I throw far and hurl my dart as far beyond others as Xenocrates had a temper sweet beyond that of other men. He was gracious in his dealings with the citizens, and practised horsebreeding in the customary manner of the Greeks; he celebrated all the customary banquets of the gods;

and the fame of his hospitality stretched from the Black Sea

[1] Son of Asopodorus, who is presumably to be identified with the Theban cavalry officer who fought at Plataea (Herodotus IX, 69).

[2] Much later in the fifth century, Alcibiades makes a similar claim (Thucydides VI, 16) and makes the benefit conferred by athletic success much more explicit. See below, pp. 142 f.

to Egypt. Even if envious hopes (presumably for Thrasybulus' downfall, Xenocrates being now dead) lurk in the minds of mortal men, Thrasybulus should not fear to proclaim his father Xenocrates' *arete*, nor to have Pindar's ode performed.

This is a fine sketch of *arete* manifested in peacetime; and if we set these two quotations together, praise is directed towards *arete* manifested in the games, in war, and in sumptuous expenditure. The effects are rather difficult to estimate. On the one hand, the *agathos*' attention is perhaps directed to these aspects of *arete* rather than to competitive success in domestic politics, so that an 'average *agathos*' might devote less thought to worsting other *agathoi* in the political sphere, or even to politics at all. (Xenocrates, of course, is already the brother of a tyrant, but the same words might be addressed to an 'average *agathos*'.) On the other hand, the praise and high esteem of the citizens derived from such sources could readily be translated into political power, as the case of Alcibiades shows; and should he feel himself in any way disadvantaged in politics, the *agathos* would be drawn by his *arete* to compete in the manner described by Darius above, even did he not regard himself, as most *agathoi* traditionally did, as qualified, *qua agathos*, to take part in politics. Furthermore, none of Pindar's praise of *arete* is concerned with justice or co-operative excellences in general. Nor can it be; for such excellences are not yet characteristically *arete*;[1] and *arete* and *eudaimonia* are still more important than mere injustice.

Can the *agathos* be restrained from the pursuit of success through injustice by the envy, *phthonos*, of his fellows? The examples quoted above show that the *agathos*, simply in virtue of his success, suffers from the *phthonos* of others, most probably, as I have already argued, other *agathoi* who find their *arete* dimmed by his shining triumphs. In a sense, therefore, *phthonos* is simply the tribute that failure pays to success;[2] and the *agathos* understands this. In Herodotus (III, 52) Periander, tyrant of Corinth, thus appeals to his son Lycophron, whom he

---

[1] For a rare exception, see below, p. 94.

[2] Pindar (*Pythians* I, 85, cited on p. 114 below) affirms the proverbial truth that it is better to be envied than pitied.

had at first driven from his household, but is now attempting to persuade to return, seeing him reduced to poverty:

My son, which is the more choiceworthy, your present condition or the tyranny and *agatha* (good things) which I possess, and which it is appropriate that you should inherit from me your father? You, who are my son and ruler of Corinth, that *eudaimon* (prosperous) city, have chosen the life of a beggar, and are setting yourself in anger against him whom you least ought to oppose. . . . But do you learn how much better it is to experience *phthonos* than pity, and at the same time how serious a matter it is to be angry with your parents and with those who are more *agathoi* than yourself, and come away to the *oikiā* (household).

Lycophron's hatred for his father is powerful enough to override these arguments; but he is certainly not deterred by fear of *phthonos* in itself; and no Greek would have held that it was better to be pitied than envied, for the most powerful values of the society drew him on to succeed, *phthonos* or no. Only if *phthonos* could find expression in hostile action to bring the *agathos* crashing down would it be a deterrent; and since *phthonos* is felt for success rather than injustice, it is sooner an inducement to the *agathos* to be wary in protecting himself against his enemies than to abstain from injustice. Certainly the *phthonos* of mankind is no more effective than fear of human reprisals in itself; and it has no particular reference to justice.

There remains the *phthonos* of the gods. Since the gods must reward and punish in this life—for the dominant view of Hades is, as it was in Homer, that the dead have a shadowy neutral existence—divine *phthonos* must manifest itself in this life in the fall of the *agathos*; and it is only manifested if the *agathos* in fact falls. Again, it is only manifested when he falls. While he succeeds, the gods are evidently on his side: Aeschylus (*Seven against Thebes* 772 ff.) can speak of the gods as favouring Oedipus while he was the prosperous ruler of Thebes, even in a context in which the speakers already know what subsequently befell Oedipus. This is to be expected, for the gods were then furnishing Oedipus with the blessings of

78

this life, and the next life has none, and no punishments: they must have been showing favour.

Accordingly, to fear the *phthonos* of the gods is to fear actual disaster. To discover the extent to which such fear is a deterrent from injustice, or from any other activity, it will be illuminating to consider the story of Croesus, King of Lydia, the richest man known to the Greeks, who evidently had a powerful claim to be regarded as most *agathos* and most *eudaimon*, and so to embody the Greek ideals of human existence. Croesus, in the tale told by Herodotus (I, 30 ff.), thought himself most *olbios*— a virtual synonym for *eudaimon*—for he was the richest man in the world. Solon, however, did not agree, but named Tellus, an Athenian. He came from a prosperous city; his children were *kaloi kāgathoi*,[1] and all survived him; and being well off for possessions, by Greek standards, he had a most glorious death, for in a battle against the Eleusinians he routed the enemy, died in a manner most *kalōs*, and was accorded a public funeral by the Athenians on the place where he died, and great honours. Second Solon placed the Argives Cleobis and Bito. They had a sufficient livelihood and sufficient strength both to be prizewinners at the games and, on their mother having to attend a festival of Hera 45 stades distant, and the oxen not coming from the fields in time, to haul their mother there themselves in the wagon. On their arrival, their mother in gratitude prayed for whatever is most *agathon* for a human being to attain; and they went to sleep in the temple and died. The Argives made and dedicated statues of them at Delphi, on the grounds that they had been *aristoi* men.

Now evidently here, despite the personalised form of expression, we are not primarily concerned with 'the most *olbios* man in the world' and 'the second most *olbios* man in the world'; but with two life-types, the most *olbios* and the second most *olbios*. Tellus represents the prosperous *agathos* of a prosperous Greek city, who achieves the height of military glory by giving his life bravely in a glorious victory which he did much himself to achieve. Cleobis and Bito, likewise of a solidly wealthy family, show familial piety, and manifest their

[1] Presumably they had every good quality that children of a man of Tellus' station in life were expected to have.

strength in a superhuman feat while displaying it. The facets of their lives that are picked out all display their possession of competitive excellences, even in a context of piety (it was their mother who wanted to go to the festival); and it is *arete* that both are manifesting—an *arete* that is to win them abundant fame after death, in the case of Cleobis and Bito a fame confirmed by statues dedicated in the most famous shrine in Greece.

Croesus cannot understand why mere 'private citizens' are to be held more *olbioi* than the richest ruler in the world. Solon replies that heaven is given to *phthonos* and to causing confusion; that anything may happen; that man is entirely chance, that his fortunes are contingent. He concedes that Croesus is wealthy and a king over many people; but he declines to call him happy, *olbios*, until he learns that he has died *kalōs*. For the very wealthy man is not more *olbios* than he who has enough for the day, unless he should have the fortune to end his life *eu*, well, in possession of all things *kala*. Many very wealthy men are not *olbioi*; and many who have a moderate livelihood enjoy good fortune. The wealthy man who is not *olbios* has advantages over the man of good fortune: he can fulfil his desires, and is better able to bear up against disaster when it comes. But the man of good fortune has every other advantage, for his good fortune keeps disaster from his door: he is unmaimed, suffers from no diseases, has no experience of *kaka*, is fortunate in his children and handsome; and if in addition he ends his life *eu*, with all good fortune, he is the person whom Croesus is seeking, the truly *olbios*; but one cannot call him *olbios* till he is dead,[1] merely 'fortunate'. Now no mere mortal can possess every kind of life's *agatha*: one must term *olbios* him who has most of them and continues to enjoy them till his death. 'One must consider the end of every affair: the god gives *olbos* to many people and then utterly overturns them.'

Now we must carefully note what Herodotus' Solon—not Solon himself—is saying here. Not that if one has a modest competence and a clear conscience one is happier than a monarch with a guilty conscience: there is no mention of

[1] For the sentiment, cf. Sophocles, *Oedipus Tyrannus*, 1528 ff.

co-operative excellences, no suggestion that Tellus was more just than Croesus; and *olbios* does not mean 'happy', while guilty consciences—as opposed to fear of punishment for wrongdoing—do not trouble the early Greeks.[1] Not that if one has a modest competence and is just the gods will keep him safe from harm, whereas the unjust monarch will be punished; for reasons already given. Simply that the gods are wont to upset one's applecart without warning, with the result that a life cannot be evaluated until it is over. (It is not even explicitly stated here that the prosperous are more likely to incur *phthonos*.) The very wealthy man *is* more *olbios* than the man who has only enough for the day, provided he has the other blessings of the *agathos*—strength, health, beauty, and children similarly endowed. Had Croesus continued in his position to the end of his life, enjoying all his *agatha*, he would have been the most *olbios*. (Tellus, Cleobis and Bito being dead, their accounts can be made up.)

This Croesus-story, presenting the gods as amoral and capricious, gives one little help in leading one's life in such a manner as to continue *olbios*, and certainly does not restrain anyone from pursuing *olbos* in an unjust manner, since the gods apparently raise up and cast down with no regard for human justice. The story might induce the fortunate to help the unfortunate, lest they themselves should one day stand in need of like help (compare *Odyssey* XVIII, 130 ff.); but it can do no more. Other stories, such as that of Polycrates and his ring, associate the *phthonos* of heaven with excessive prosperity (Herodotus III, 40 ff.); but since this folk-tale depicts Polycrates as unable to rid himself of prosperity, and so doomed, it would be difficult to base practical advice on it.

These stories reflect the real anxieties of the prosperous. Living in an environment of whose natural and economic laws they knew little, they might at any time be struck by inexplicable disaster; and, partly for this very reason, accepting myths many of which represented the gods, to whom they ascribed their successes and failures, as capricious or malevolent, how could they not live in a state of anxiety?

[1] For *miasma*, 'pollution'—which is not to be identified with moral guilt—see *Merit and Responsibility*, chapter v, and especially pp. 94 ff.

However, since in this belief the gods are not held to be just, the *agathos* is not urged by it to be just in an effort to avoid disaster. When Bacchylides (31 (3), 83) says to the tyrant Hiero

'Do *hosia* and cheer your heart; for this is the greatest of benefits,' it is inadvisable to render, with the Loeb Classical Library translator, 'Cheer then thy heart by righteous deeds'. To do *hosia* is to do what the gods desire; and where the gods do not desire righteousness, piety does not entail righteousness. The context makes the meaning clear. Bacchylides has been singing of Croesus, who was a very generous benefactor of Delphi and other oracular shrines. Apollo should evidently have been grateful, and have shielded Croesus from harm; for even when believed to be unconcerned with the justice and injustice of mortals to each other, the gods are supposed to show gratitude for favours received.[1] Now the fall of Croesus, in this sense a highly 'pious' person, set great problems for Delphi, the chief beneficiary, and its god Apollo; and it is possible to discern mighty efforts to show that Croesus did benefit from his 'piety': both Herodotus (I, 87) and Bacchylides, whose versions are greatly influenced by Delphi, here maintain that Croesus was saved from the pyre by Apollo (or Zeus and Apollo); and Herodotus adds (I, 91) that Croesus was expiating the sins of his ancestor Gyges, committed five generations before, and that Apollo had done his best and had indeed persuaded the Moirai to postpone for three years the capture of Sardis. So Croesus was rewarded, says Bacchylides (61 f.),

> On account of his *eusebeia*, in that he had, more than any other mortal, sent gifts to goodly Pytho.

Croesus' *eusebeia*, his 'piety', is his sending of gifts to Apollo's oracle; and for this he expects great recompense. The greater

[1] This belief is never fully harmonised with the belief that the gods may be capricious and malevolent. The Greek hopes for due return for his sacrifices and offerings, and may complain if due return is not made, as Croesus complains (Herodotus I, 90); but he can never have been entirely confident that the gods would keep their side of the bargain.

the gifts, the greater the favours to be hoped for in return; for the poem continues (63 f.):

> Yet, illustrious Hiero, no man of those who (now) hold Greece in sway will claim that he has sent more gold to Apollo than you have.

The argument is clear: 'You are not so rich as Croesus; yet you have given more gold to Apollo than has any other Greek; accordingly, you are more *eusebēs* and may expect more in return.' The implications of 'Do *hosia* and cheer your heart' are thus evident: 'Continue to give gifts to Apollo; and you may then have many more years of wealthy life.'

The belief may allay the anxieties of the tyrant; but it is not specially designed for this purpose. From Homer onwards, one strand of belief portrays the gods as moved solely by sacrifice and the dedication of valuable objects—and prayer, reminding the god of sacrifices offered and dedications made; and a necessary corollary of any such belief is usually that one's *eusebeia* is proportional to one's pocket-book. Euripides (Nauck² frag. 946) speaks out against it:

> Be assured that when any man who is *eusebes* sacrifices to the gods, he secures his safety even if the sacrifice is a small one.

The use of *eusebes* here is quite different from that of Bacchylides, but the behaviour of Croesus and Hiero towards non-moral gods has an equally good claim to be termed *eusebeia*. (Euripides' usage is related to the belief that deities are concerned with justice, which will be discussed below.) All Greeks worshipped the gods with sacrifice; and the natural assumption to make was that the larger the sacrifice, the greater would be the resulting favour of the gods. There is little inducement here to be just rather than prosperous, if a choice must be made; as Adeimantus (Plato, *Republic* II, 362C) says, in enumerating the advantages which popular opinion ascribes to the unjust:

> . . . and ⟨the unjust⟩ does service to the gods . . . far better than the just ⟨since he is more prosperous⟩ . . . so that he

83

may reasonably expect to be more dear to the gods than is the just man.

The conclusion follows directly from a belief in such gods; and it is hardly an inducement to be just.

However, this belief does not exclude others: at all times the Greek religious landscape is characterised by variety. It is evident that Greek deities sometimes brought to disaster mortals who had displayed *hubris*, though we have seen that in the sixth century an action could be termed *hubris* without regarding divine reprisals as inevitable. We must now consider the fifth-century belief, examining not only this question but also the nature and function of the concept of *hubris* in the light of the full range of types of passage in which it occurs. By tacitly assuming that a god's disapproval of an action must be based on its being a breach of what we should regard as justice, and confining our attention to a small and possibly untypical selection of famous passages, we may be completely misled.[1] In Bacchylides (10, 50 ff.) Menelaus says:

> Warriors of Troy, all-seeing Zeus who reigns on high is not the cause of great woes for mortals. No; all mankind may readily attain to 'straight' . . . *dike* (justice) that accompanies *eunomia* the pure and wise right; and *olbioi* are they whose children choose her to dwell with them. But brazen *hubris* who flourishes on slippery gains and unseemly follies, and quickly grants to a man wealth and power that belong to another, and then sends him to deep disaster—*hubris* it was that destroyed the overproud sons of Earth, the giants.

Here *hubris* is opposed to justice and *eunomia*. The latter, as we have seen, commends, or has overtones of, a 'good' apportionment of the city's resources, while also commending a condition where the laws are either 'good' ones, or properly enforced, or both. Different Greeks might have had different views on the nature of a 'good' apportionment or 'good' laws; but our sources are predominantly prosperous writers,

[1] The points made in the subsequent paragraphs are, I believe, relevant also to the sixth century; but the more fragmentary nature of the sixth century evidence makes demonstration more difficult.

agathoi, so that the word in our texts has a predominantly 'right-wing' or 'conservative' flavour, and *may* have been exclusively a watchword of the *agathoi*. (To say this is not, of course, to say that *eunomia means* 'a state of affairs in which the *agathoi* have all the advantages': *eunomia* commends a state of affairs which the speaker regards as 'best for the city', which, not surprisingly, will frequently be the state of affairs most advantageous for himself. Similarly, *dikaiosune* commends what is fair and just, and does not *mean* 'what is in my own interest'; but, as Thrasymachus pointed out (Plato, *Republic* I, 338D ff.), groups in a society not infrequently regard as fair and just what is in fact in their own interest, and 'justify' the claim by introducing criteria which render it fair for them to have the advantage. *Dikaiosune*, however, does commend in intention an objective standard of fairness: two Greeks can dispute whether a course of action is just without each concerning himself with the question whether it is to his own advantage or, if one is the stronger, more *agathos*, whether it is to the stronger's advantage.) Accordingly, to oppose *hubris* to justice is to give the word in this context the appearance of simply decrying breaches of co-operative excellences; but the association with *eunomia*, and with the transgressions of the giants, whose misdeeds constituted not simply injustice, but rather 'getting above themselves', may lead us to doubt whether *hubris* decries as an act of injustice an act which we ourselves might regard in this manner. (Menelaus' words are a generalisation, not wholly applicable to his situation, which is not concerned with gain and loss of power: we may infer that the lines have general social and political relevance.)

In a different kind of context, the ghost of Darius says (Aeschylus, *Persians* 821 ff.), referring to the disaster of the Persian army,

> For *hubris* has flowered and borne a crop of *ate* (disaster) whence it is reaping a harvest of woe.

One ought not to have overproud thoughts when one is a mortal (820). Accordingly (823 ff.),

> Seeing then that such are the penalties for these things, remember Athens and Greece, and let no-one, despising his

present fortune, be struck with desire for more and lose great *olbos*. For Zeus, a heavy chastiser, is near as a punisher of minds that boast too much.

The chorus should counsel Xerxes on his return to cease from behaving with infatuate and overboastful daring.

In the lines quoted, the disaster is a requital for aiming at excessive prosperity, so that the motive of the gods is presumably *phthonos*. Earlier in the same speech, however, *hubris* and 'impious thoughts' (808 ff.) led the Persians to destroy the temples of the gods in Greece: an offence against divine property and *time*. In neither case are the Persians being punished for acts of injustice: indeed, the attack on Greece might be represented—and is represented by Xerxes and Mardonius (Herodotus, VII, 8 and 9)—as a just reprisal for the mainland Greeks' support of the Ionians in their revolt against Persia. The Persians have not necessarily acted unjustly; but they have 'got above themselves'.

In other cases, human beings are affronted by the *hubris*. In Sophocles (*Antigone* 477 ff.) Creon says of Antigone:

> I know that spirited horses are checked by a small bit; for it does not befit anyone to *mega phronein* (be haughty) who is the slave of those about him. She was already versed in *hubrizein* in transgressing the established laws; and now that she has done the deed, here is a second act of *hubris*: she laughs!

Similarly, Clytemnestra says of Electra (Sophocles, *Electra*, 612 ff.)

> What attitude should I have to this girl, who has *hubrizein* her own mother in this manner, and that too though she is still young?

For Antigone, in Creon's eyes, it is *hubris* to transgress the established laws, and *hubris* to take the attitude that she has taken to the deed. Electra has just (558 ff.) delivered a long indictment of Clytemnestra's actions and motives; and the chorus (610 f.) wondered briefly whether or no right was on Electra's side. Clytemnestra ignores this question: for a child thus to rebuke its mother, whatever crimes the mother has committed, is *hubris*, 'getting above itself'. Evidently Creon too, despite the mention of laws, thus evaluates Antigone's actions, for she, who is in his eyes virtually his slave, has 'got above herself'. Now we may say that Sophocles himself is opposed to the views represented by Clytemnestra and Creon; but he is evidently opposing attitudes which exist in the society, and which follow directly from traditional evaluations.[1]

Hubris, then, may be used to censure a human being, naturally usually an *agathos*, who has been impelled—by his *arete*—to transgress the limits of what the gods permit to men; and also within families, where it might well be used to restrain the younger from striving for justice or their rights. Similarly, in politics, the idea is available to the *agathoi* as a means of suppressing opposition. It may be held—by the *agathoi*—to be *hubris* to strive against the *agathoi* for political power or for one's political rights, as seems indicated by Pindar, *Pythian* IV, when Demophilus is praised (281 ff.):

> He, a youth among the young but in his counsels like an elder of one hundred years old, bereaves slander of her brilliant voice, and has learned to hate *hubris*, not striving against the *agathoi* . . .

Demophilus himself is a man of means and position—he commissioned *Pythian* IV, the longest and most splendid Pindaric ode—who has been exiled; but the sentiment is general, and would serve to convict of *hubris* any social inferior who endeavoured to assert his rights against an *agathos*. Similarly, the Egyptians (Herodotus VII, 5) as revolted subjects are held to be displaying *hubris* towards the Persians.

To stand up for one's rights, of course, in the sense of asserting that one's rights should be equal with those of the more powerful, or at all events should be greater than they are, is to upset the present distribution of rights and privileges in a society, like that of ancient Greece at this time, where the distribution is unequal. 'Justice' may well be used to commend the status quo; and certainly *hubris* may be used to decry any attempt to depart from it, for *hubris* belongs to a group of

[1] Cf. Teucer in Sophocles' *Ajax*, above, pp. 65 ff.

ideas, found already in Homer, which favour the status quo.
Important in this group are *aisa* and *moira*; and any rendering
of these by 'Fate', a rendering frequent in the translators,
completely misrepresents the thought of the Greek.

In Aeschylus (*Suppliant Women* 670 ff.) the Chorus prays:

> Thus may their city be *nemesthai* (regulated) *eu* (well) if
> they revere mighty Zeus, and especially Zeus protector of
> guests, who guides *aisa* aright by an age-old law, *nomos*.

The usual rendering of *aisa* seems to be 'destiny', the relevance
of which to the context is not very clear. Earlier in the play,
however, the Chorus had prayed (78 ff.)

> But, gods of our race, give ear and look well upon the
> *dikaion* (the cause of justice). If you prevent youth from
> fulfilling its desires that are in contravention of *aisa*,
> and truly abhor *hubris*, you would be *endikoi* (righteous) towards
> marriage.

There *aisa* is rendered 'what is right' or something similar, as
in Homer.[1] But *aisa* is the same word in both passages, and
has the same implications. In 670 ff. Zeus is to 'guide *aisa*
aright' and maintain the due apportionments, 'shares', as a
result of which the city is to be well-regulated, *eu nemesthai*, the
roots of the phrase being those of *eunomia*. The existing apportionment of 'shares', rights, privileges, status is, as in Homer,
assumed by many to be the correct one, and *all* transgressions
against it will be seen in terms of *hubris*, of 'getting above oneself', of 'crossing the boundaries of one's share', of 'trespass'.
Some such transgressions will be ethical in our eyes, as when
the sons of Aegyptus wish to marry the Danaids against their
will in the *Suppliant Women*. Some will not, as in the cases of
Antigone, Electra and Demophilus. But all when characterised as *hubris*, acting against *aisa*, are thereby classified together; all are deterred with the same sanction; and once
again the field of ethics is confused with other fields, where a
desire for political change can be treated in the same way as an
act of injustice. Both are disapproved of by society, or its most
powerful members; and both are disapproved of in the same

[1] See p. 19 f. *Moira* and *aisa* are synonymous.

88

way. So, in the *Eumenides*, the Chorus (961 ff.) thus apostrophise the *Moirai*:

> Grant it, O divine *Moirai*, our sisters from the same mother, *orthonomoi* (divinities whose apportionment is correct), who have a part in every household, and who at all times are grievous, and most honoured by reason of their just visitations.

The *Moirai* are here quasi-personified; but the function of the 'share' is the same: it is the *moirai* who grant to each his appropriate status and position, and punish those who seek to vary it by whatever means. (The rôle of justice will be considered below.)

If we turn to the individual, we can find illuminating remarks made by Aeschylean characters about the manner in which his position was evaluated. In the *Prometheus Bound*, Oceanus says (288 ff.):

> For your situation, be assured, I feel sympathy. My kinship with you, I think, constrains me to this; and, quite apart from kinship, there is no-one to whom I would allot a greater *moira* than to you.

Similarly, in the *Libation-Bearers*, Electra thus addresses her newly-found brother Orestes (238 ff.):

> O . . . you who have four *moirai* in my eyes, for I must call you father, and the love belonging to my mother—whom I justly hate—comes to you, as does the love for my sister who was cruelly sacrificed.

Orestes receives not only his own *moira* from his sister, but also the *moirai* of Agamemnon, Clytemnestra and Iphigenia. To allot someone a *moira*—as Oceanus puts it—or to acknowledge his possession of a *moira* gives him status in one's eyes, gives him claims upon one. The totality, the system of *moirai*, under the guardianship of gods, whether *moirai* personified, Zeus or others, constitutes a stratified system—stratified, since *moirai* differ from each other—of rights, privileges and status; and since the established system of *moirai* in a traditionalist society is held to be the right system, the right manner of distributing shares, to wish to vary it, by whatever means, may be censured in the same manner, as *hubris*.

To term an action *hubris*, then, is neither to express the belief that it will undoubtedly be punished, nor yet to censure it in a manner which a modern reader would be likely to regard as exclusively ethical. What, then, of actions evaluated in terms of *dike* or *dikaiosune*? In speaking of justice, we are accustomed to think of equality before the law, and assume that in any society man or god must associate justice with equal rights for poor and rich, weak and strong, *kakos* and *agathos*. In Sophocles' *Ajax* (above, pp. 65 ff.) we have seen Teucer, with *dike* on his side, attempting to assert his just claim in the teeth of the claims of *arete* (though as we have seen, he also asserts that his fighting prowess is the equal of Menelaus'). But surely, we may say, in states with written laws there was equality before the law. Here, as the next chapter will show, there may be a distinction between theory and practice; but this is undoubtedly the purpose of the written law which applies penalties to 'the wrongdoer' rather than different penalties to *agathos* and *kakos*. However, the gods do not punish in court, nor in terms of written laws; and in many contexts where the gods are spoken of as defending *dike*, it is against *hubris* that they defend it; so that *dike* may well, in these contexts and in others in which *hubris* is not explicitly mentioned, require that one should remain within the bounds of the traditional *moira*-structure. We have seen (above, p. 88) the Chorus in Aeschylus' *Suppliant Women* asking the gods of their race to defend 'the *dikaion*' against *hubris* and what is contrary to *aisa*; and Menelaus opposing *hubris* to *dike* in what appears to be a context of possible socio-political upheaval. The justice that the gods uphold may not be always what we should suppose.

Nevertheless, there is a general tendency for justice to separate itself from the claims of the old *moira*-system; and this is indeed dramatically represented in an extant work. One of the many motifs in that richest of dramatic tapestries, the Orestes-trilogy, is the successful opposition of law-court justice, here represented as the justice of the Olympians, to the old distribution of *moirai*, which allotted to the Erinyes the function of haunting certain individuals—for example, matricides—without the possibility of considering motive or circumstances. Now by the time Aeschylus wrote the Orestes-trilogy there had been homicide and other courts in Athens for many years; so that there is no immediate relevance in the change from Erinyes-haunting to trial before a court. But (setting on one side the political allusions that have been plausibly discovered in the *Eumenides*) the Athens of Aeschylus' day, rapidly being democratised in institutions, was indeed upsetting the traditional *moirai* of society and *attempting* to move in the direction of equality before the law. Aeschylus, as ever, is difficult to interpret: he offers no easy solution to the complexities of Greek beliefs, but he is moving in a definite direction. Consider a few passages of the *Eumenides*. At 169 ff. the Chorus says to Apollo:

> Seer though you are, you, self-sped and self-summoned, have defiled the recesses of your shrine with pollution at your own hearth, giving honour to human affairs against the *nomos* of the gods and having destroyed the *moirai* that were born long ago.

And at 333 ff.:

> The unswerving *moira* span this allotted task for me to have unceasingly, that I should consort with those mortals who are concerned with rash murders of their own kin until they pass beneath the earth; and even when dead such a one is not over-free.

The Erinyes have a *moira*, which endows them with rights, status and functions that are unaffected by circumstances, and which it is right that they should have: it is their *moira* and their *time*. When Orestes is pronounced to have acted justly, they say that they are *atimoi* (780); to which Athena replies that they should not grieve too much, for (795)

> You have not been defeated. No; *dike* with an equal number of votes has come out honestly, not from *atimia* of you. But from Zeus there was clear witness. . . .

When the Erinyes have been pacified, Athena says (973)

> But Zeus, god of the *agora* (gathering, court) has prevailed.

The implication is that the justice of the court has prevailed over the requirements of *moira*: that appropriate treatment is to be determined in terms of criteria other than status and position in family or city; but immediately before this the Chorus sang 961 ff., quoted above, which indicate the rôle of the *moirai* in fixing the status and position of each—a rôle which is not essentially modified in the *Eumenides*: the Furies have been won over when they sing these lines, which proclaim a state of affairs which is to continue for the future. Equality is not evidently to carry the day: Aeschylus, 'advanced' for his day, is a cautious reformer, like Solon before him.

But whatever it is that the gods are to punish, *hubris* or *adikia*, and however *adikia* is to be interpreted, there is a strong thread of belief at this period that the gods punish certain human deeds; and the belief is necessary if the co-operative excellences, however interpreted in detail, are to be valued. The Erinyes surely speak for Aeschylus and many of his contemporaries when they say (517 ff.):

There is a place[1] for *to deinon* (what is terrible): it should remain enthroned as a watcher over the *phrenes* (mind). It is profitable to *sōphronein* (be prudent, self-controlled) with groaning. Who that, in the 'light' of his heart, trembles at nothing, would continue to reverence *dike* (justice) in like manner ⟨as in the past⟩?

Approve neither a life of anarchy nor one subject to a master. The god gives power to moderation in every form. The word that I utter has due proportion: *hubris* is in truth the child of impiety; but, from health of *phrenes*[2] (mind) comes *olbos* dear to all and much sought for in prayer.

And in general I say to you; revere the altar of *dike*; and do not kick it in dishonour with godless foot; for punishment will come to you. The end that is decreed awaits. Therefore let a man give the most honour and respect to his

[1] Literally, 'there is a place where *to deinon*, what is terrible, is well, *eu*'.

[2] The implications of the phrase resemble those of *sōphronein*. The views expressed here should be compared with Solon 6, above, p. 51.

parents, and show reverence for the stranger within his gates with due hospitality.

He who of his own free will, without compulsion, is *dikaios* shall not be without *olbos*, and would never perish utterly; but the defiant transgressor with his great freight piled up with no thought of justice shall in time be compelled to haul down his sail, when the stress of tempest seizes him and the yardarm is shattered.

He calls upon those who do not hear, and he struggles in vain amid the swirling waters. The god laughs at the reckless man who boasted that this would never happen, helpless as he now is as a result of his woes that have no cure and unable to surmount the crest of the waves; and having wrecked the *olbos* he had before throughout his life on the reef of justice he perishes unwept and unperceived.

Here we have, bluntly stated, the means necessary to restrain the *agathos* from committing injustice or *hubris*: the gods must ensure that such behaviour does not pay. The vehemence of the statement at so pivotal a point of the *Oresteia* doubtless indicates that Aeschylus felt that his fellow-citizens were in danger of ceasing to believe that the gods effectively discharged this function: the attitudes which will be discussed in the next chapter were already developing, as they might well develop when the Athenians began to realise their new political importance and effectiveness in the Greek world, and to develop from it a wide-ranging confidence. Nevertheless, the first lesson learned from the Persian Wars, as we can see from the work of both Aeschylus and Herodotus, was that the gods had humbled the mighty and brought *hubris* to naught; and until this lesson had grown dim, and the Athenians began to feel confidence based on their own might, Aeschylus' words of restraint might prove effective in foreign and domestic politics and in personal relationships alike.

Where *arete* retains its traditional characteristics, such restraints are necessary. Were *dikaiosune* to become part of *arete*, however, it would become choiceworthy; for *aretai* are choiceworthy *per se*. Theognis, as we have seen,[1] once asserted

[1] Above, p. 42.

that *dikaiosune* was the whole of *arete*; but part would suffice. Theognis' words seem to have no effect on the extant literature of the earlier fifth century. In Aeschylus, it is true, *kakos* can be used in generalisations to decry the unjust (*Suppliant Women* 402 ff.); but it is not used to decry particular individuals for their injustice, and *agathos* is not used to commend the co-operative excellences at all. The often-cited line praising Amphiaraus (*Seven against Thebes* 610) as

Sōphrōn, dikaios, agathos and pious,

which is said to demonstrate that *arete* may commend co-operative excellences for Aeschylus, in fact demonstrates the contrary. *Agathos* is the adjective which corresponds in range to *arete*; and clearly being *sophron* and *dikaios* is distinct from being *agathos* in Aeschylus' mind; so that they are evidently not part of *arete* at this period. The nearest approach to an assertion that *dikaiosune* is a part of *arete* occurs in Timocreon, the Rhodian lyric and elegiac poet (fragment 1). The author praises Aristides as *lōistos*, most *agathos*, in sharp contrast with Themistocles,

The liar, the unjust, the traitor who, persuaded by a bribe of knavish silver coins, did not bring back Timocreon, though he was his *xeinos*, from exile to his native Ialysus.

He rejects the claims of Pausanias, Xanthippus and Leotychides, all successful military commanders in the Persian Wars, as well as those of Themistocles, also a successful commander, to be most *agathos*; and favours instead Aristides, best known to us for his renowned justice. It may be tempting to see in this a new up-valuing of co-operative excellences. However, Aristides' justice is not explicitly mentioned; and Timocreon's complaint is that Themistocles has not brought him back from exile *though he was his xeinos*. To fail to forward the interests of one's *xeinoi*, whether wilfully or from incapacity, shows a deficiency in *arete* from earliest times: Timocreon's complaint is thus far couched in terms of traditional values. Furthermore, it is evident (fragment 3) that Timocreon was kept in exile as a collaborator with the Persians: it seems likely that Themistocles was preferring to the claims of guest-friendship

94

those of Greek patriotism, also evaluated in terms of traditional *arete*, but, in the period of the Persian Wars, applied over a new and larger field.[1] At all events, pique plays a sufficiently large part in Timocreon's judgment to render it difficult to regard it as a considered revaluation.

We have here, most unusually, the verbal usage of a member of a state now beginning to be faced with an active Athens stronger than itself, and soon to become expansionist. Again, in the Persian Wars, *agathoi* Greeks found themselves very much in the weaker position before an enemy much stronger than themselves. The experience might perhaps have been expected to lead to new evaluations; but there is little indication of it at this period: even the feeling of Greek unity soon evaporated.

Within individual cities, the relationship between competitive values and civil discord is little understood. Bacchylides (48) says:

Mortals do not themselves choose either *olbos* or inexorable Ares (War) or all-destructive civil strife. No; *aisa* that gives all brings down a cloud now on this land, now on that.

It is evident that Bacchylides sees no link between competitive excellences and the resulting civil strife: if civil strife is a city's 'lot', civil strife it will have. No co-operative *arete* is likely to develop until its contribution to civic well-being is recognised.

One last mode of restraint is possible. As we have seen, most articulate Greeks whose views are recorded for us believed that this life is all, and that all good and ill fortune, all reward and punishment, must occur while we live. There is, however, another belief, attested for the first time in the 'Homeric' *Hymn to Demeter*, whose date may be early sixth century, for which the evidence, though still scanty and scattered, becomes a little more available in the fifth century. In this belief, the *psūchē*, or shade, of the dead enjoys a more real existence, and different *psuchai* may have different lots after death. The means whereby a better lot may be obtained vary. The belief seems to take its rise from the mystery-cults; and here it is not surprising to find Bliss offered as a reward for merely having been initiated. In the *Hymn to Demeter* we have (480 ff.):

[1] Above, p. 58 f.

Blessed is he among men upon earth who has seen these things; but he who is not initiated and has no part in the rites never has a share of such good things when he is dead in the gloomy darkness.

The belief occurs in scattered references in the fifth century;[1] and the Eleusinian Mysteries, the subject of the reference in the *Hymn to Demeter*, together with many other mystery-cults,[2] flourished thereafter throughout pagan antiquity. Where initiation *per se* guarantees Bliss, the moral effect is nil; but though the nature of the 'things' seen was a secret, and varied from cult to cult, the promise of a more 'real' life after death was not secret; and the belief, where it existed, was available to the moralist. In Aeschylus we find two uses of the belief to deter from injustice. In the *Suppliant Women* Danaus maintains that no man who forced marriage on his daughters would be pure, but that even when dead he would have to pay a penalty (228 ff.):

In the next world, it is said, another Zeus pronounces final judgment among the dead for wrongdoing.

In the *Eumenides*, too, the Furies threaten that they will wither Orestes and carry him off to Hades to be punished for his matricide. They add (269 ff.):

There you will see all other mortals who have impiously wronged a god, some guest-friend or their dear parents, each receiving his deserved punishment. For Hades is a mighty judge of mortals beneath the earth, and he watches everything with faithfully recording mind.

In such passages as these Hades, the 'other Zeus', is believed

[1] See Pindar, *Laments for the Dead* frag. 137 (102); and for later material, but material which probably reflects earlier belief and practice, 'Orpheus' frags. 17–20 Diels/Kranz.

[2] Mystery-cults offered to their members a better lot after death than was offered by the dank and shadowy Hades of the mainstream of Greek religion. Initiation was necessary; the rites were secret; and terrible oaths of secrecy were demanded, with the result that the nature of the rites is still a matter of speculation among scholars.

to punish in the next world the injustices which it is hoped that Zeus will punish in this, and which he all too frequently fails to punish. In the next world, however, there can be no escape, and punishment falls, not upon the descendants, but upon the wrongdoer himself. In so far as it is held, surely this belief must be a powerful inducement to be just.

What must be set on the other side? In the first place, among those Greeks of whose beliefs we have any knowledge, this belief plays little part. Beliefs in the rest of society, and in cities other than Athens, can usually only be guessed at. Democritus (Diels/Kranz B199 and B297) speaks as though fear of punishment after death blighted the lives of many; and this may have been true in cities of which we know nothing. But the non-moral belief in initiation as a ticket to Bliss must have been more widespread than the moral belief; and even here the evidence is problematical. The Athenian state sponsored the Eleusinian mysteries, which were deeply reverenced by the Athenians, and propagated belief in salvation through initiation; yet in orations over men dead in war, where the audience must be a large one, drawn from much of the citizen-body, the 'Homeric' view of the next life is characteristic.[1]

The belief in a moral Last Judgment seems likely to have been that of a minority of all Greeks; while the presence of the non-moral belief of the mysteries[2] must have once again confused moral with non-moral considerations. The undogmatic nature of Greek religion has its part to play here too: even in those writers, Aeschylus and Pindar, who express the moral belief, it appears but rarely: the general presuppositions and values of Aeschylus and Pindar are those which have been discussed elsewhere in this chapter. Pindar's views vary with those of his patrons; but Aeschylus was under no such necessity. Belief in a moral Last Judgment had little ascertainable part to play in the fifth century.

In these circumstances, the only restraint upon the pursuit of the maximum of success that appears to be within one's grasp by whatever means lie to hand, in order to maximise

[1] See for example, Demosthenes 60, 34, Lysias 2, *passim*.

[2] For a fuller discussion, see *Merit and Responsibility* pp. 140 ff., *From the Many to the One*, pp. 66 ff.

one's *eudaimonia* and display one's *arete*, must be the belief that the gods will inevitably punish such behaviour in this life. The general impression conveyed by the surviving documents of the earlier fifth century suggests that the restraint was at this time quite effective when the belief that the gods punished injustice—or *hubris*—was actually present to the mind; though the vehemence of some of Aeschylus' lines, and of Pindar's exhortations to the *agathos* to 'think mortal thoughts' must betoken at least severe strains. It is a mistake to assume, as is sometimes assumed, that societies whose moralists consistently exhort them to be moderate, or to display any other specific virtue, are societies to whom moderation, or the virtue in question, comes easily. The reverse is much more likely to be the case. At all events, belief in divine reprisals seems essential at this period to underwrite co-operative excellences (which, as we have seen, should not be hastily equated at this period with what we should term 'justice'). In the next chapter we shall discuss the results of the weakening, and in some cases vanishing, of this belief in the later fifth century.

5

The Later Fifth Century

A. INTRODUCTORY

THUS far, the *agathos* Greek has been induced to behave justly in circumstances in which, so far as his fellow human beings were concerned, injustice would have brought him greater success, by the fear of divine punishment. In so far as he believed that injustice and other breaches of co-operative excellences would be punished by the gods, he believed that any such punishment would consist in disaster, reduction in prosperity and well-being; so that the prosperity and stability of his household, which was the goal of his actions, was better secured by co-operating justly with his fellows in the city than by displaying his competitive *arete*, and ruthlessly trampling his fellow-citizens underfoot, whenever he seemed able to do so. We have seen that there were many difficulties for the Greek in the way of believing that his gods were just, and always punished in this life, or that what they punished was specifically injustice; but they offered the best hope which the weaker possessed that the stronger would be restrained from committing injustices that were within his power. The *kakos* Greek has been induced to defer to the *agathos* both by the implications of *kakos*, which decried him as an inferior specimen of human being, and also by those of *moira*, which both established his lowly station and also gave it the sanction of heaven, and rendered it *hubris* to strive for a better lot. *Moira* also established the superior status of the *agathos* in comparison with the *kakos*; and, taken by itself, it established the *agathos'* subordinate position in the face of deity; but the *agathos'* possession of *arete* also had its part to play.

Kakoi may well have deferred; but at least some *agathoi* Greeks had evidently been drawn to strive for ever greater success by the pull of *arete*, to such an extent that Pindar must be frequently reminding the *agathos* to 'think mortal thoughts'. This in the earlier fifth century; and in the later part of the fifth century human self-esteem increased. No one cause can be assigned; but among the causes is likely to have been the Greek victory in the Persian Wars. At first, as we have seen in Aeschylus and Herodotus, the lesson that the Greeks drew —or that Aeschylus and Herodotus drew—was that pride, *hubris*, is humbled by the gods; but as the Greeks grew more used to the idea that they had beaten the Persians, and the Athenians in particular benefited from the victory by obtaining a hegemony, and indeed an empire, over the Aegean islands and the seaboard of Asia Minor, they may well have been more impressed by human capacity than by divine vengeance. Space does not permit the discussion of all the possible causes of change; but among the new phenomena of this period, themselves partly assisted by the new situation and partly encouraging further developments, were the sophists, itinerant teachers of rhetoric and other politically useful skills;[1] and the sophists were characteristically agnostics. In the new intellectual climate a Sophoclean chorus can sing (*Antigone* 332 ff.):

Many are the things that are *deinon*, and none is more *deinon* than man: he crosses the grey sea, driven by the stormy south wind, making his path beneath swelling waves that tower around him; and Earth, the most august of the gods, Earth the immortal, the unwearied, does he wear, as the ploughs go to and fro from year to year, cultivating with the offspring of horses.

And he, cunning man, traps in woven nets and leads captive the race of light-hearted birds, the tribes of wild beasts and the creatures that are produced in the sea; and he overcomes by his *mēchanē* (devices) the mountain-roaming wild beast that dwells in the wilds and tames the shaggy-necked horse, putting the yoke upon its neck, and the bull of the mountain that does not grow weary.

And he has taught himself speech, and thought swift as the wind, and dispositions suited to living in cities, and how

[1] Some sophists claimed to be competent to teach virtually anything, cf. Hippias of Elis as presented in the Platonic dialogues which bear his name; but these are the skills relevant to the present discussion.

to escape the darts of the frost that strike from a clear sky, and the darts of the rain. He is all-resourceful; nothing that is to come does he meet without resource; only from death will he contrive no means of flight: from *amechanoi* (baffling) diseases he has devised means of escape.

Having, in his contriving skill, something *sophon* (clever)[1] beyond expectation, at one time he comes to *kakon*, at another to *esthlon*. When he observes the *nomoi* (laws and customs) of the land and the justice which he has sworn by the gods to uphold, high is his city; but that man who consorts with what is not *kalon* by reason of his daring—he has no city. May he who does these things never share my hearth, and may I never be of one mind with him.

This is not Sophocles' final word on the nature and status of man in the *Antigone*; but we are concerned with what is being thought and said, and accepted by many, whether Sophocles himself rejects it or no. Evidently the climate of thought is changing. In the *Eumenides*, the Furies proclaimed that the *deinon*, the terrible, served a useful purpose in restraining mankind from injustice; and they, as deities, were the source of the *deinon*. Now mankind is *deinon*, a word which spans clever and terrible; and his triumphs are his own. For Aeschylus, a mere generation before, the view of man's progress in the *Prometheus Bound* is set in the framework of the benefaction and sufferings of Prometheus, in a play in which the only human character is Io, one of Zeus' victims; and all Aeschylus' characters inhabit a world in which deities take a terrible vengeance for human actions of which, for whatever reason, they disapprove. For Sophocles' chorus here, the success and prosperity of the city depend on the observance of justice which one swears by the gods to uphold; and the closing lines express the belief that the gods may punish the group for the injustice of the individual; but the balance of emphasis in their thought has shifted towards man and away from deity.

[1] *Sophos* in Platonic and philosophical usage generally is rendered 'wise'; but in fifth-century Greek (and in non-philosophical later Greek) the word is frequently used to express something closer to cleverness.

Sophists, and the pupils of sophists, could go much further. Critias, a wealthy Athenian of high birth, a dramatist, a pupil of sophists and one of the Thirty Tyrants who took power in Athens at the end of the Peloponnesian War, puts the following lines into the mouth of one of his characters in his *Sisyphus*, a satyr-play (Diels/Kranz B25):

> There was a time when the life of man was without order, beastlike and under the dominance of strength; when there was no prize for the *esthloi* nor punishment for the *kakoi*. And then, I think, men made themselves *nomoi* as punishers, that *dike* might be tyrant and have *hubris* as her slave, and that anyone who erred might be punished. Then, when the *nomoi* restrained them from committing open and violent crimes, they committed crimes by stealth; and *then* I think that some *sophos* (shrewd and clever) man devised for mortals fear of the gods, that the *kakoi* might have some fear even if it was by stealth that they were doing, saying or devising something. For this reason, then, he introduced the idea of the divine, maintaining that there is a deity flourishing with a life that is immortal, hearing and seeing with his mind, whose thoughts are exceedingly great and whose attention is directed to mankind, who has a divine *phusis* (nature) and will hear all that is said among mortals and will be able to see all that is done. And if one silently plots some *kakon* (harm), this will not escape the notice of the gods; for their intelligence is too powerful.

The speaker seems—the context is lost—to be on the side of 'law and order';[1] but where the only effective restraint upon the pursuit of *arete* as far as one's power would allow was the belief in deities who would infallibly punish in this life, the reduction of the gods to useful fictions was unlikely to induce those Greeks who accepted it to be law-abiding citizens.[2] The career of Critias himself was not notably law-abiding.

[1] Cf. and contrast Euripides *Hecuba* 799 f., where Hecuba both states that belief in the gods depends on *nomos* and also expresses a belief in divine power.

[2] Nevertheless, *esthlos* and *kakos* are used co-operatively in this passage. See below, pp. 112 ff.

B. *Nomos* AND JUSTICE

The best-known extant passages of sophistic writing on law and society are hostile to 'law and order'; and Plato evidently regarded the sophists as one of the ills of society. This is, however, a partial view; and it may be useful to begin with some passages whose intention is quite different.

The atomist Democritus may be broadly classed with the sophists when he is concerned with ethical topics.[1] He writes (Diels/Kranz B248):

> The *nomos* wishes to benefit the life of men; and it can do so, when they themselves are willing to be benefited; for the law shows its own *arete* (excellence) to those who obey.

Protagoras, as portrayed by Plato in the dialogue which bears his name, is concerned primarily with justice rather than *nomos*. He writes (322A3 ff.):

> Since man had a share of divine *moira*, first he alone believed in gods on account of his kinship with the god, and tried to set up altars and statues to the gods; then he swiftly attained by his skill to articulate speech and words, and invented houses and clothes and shoes and bedding and agriculture. Now, thus equipped, men lived a scattered life at first, and there were no cities; and so they used to be destroyed by wild beasts because they were altogether weaker than the beasts, and the craftsman's *techne* (art, craft, skill) was sufficient aid in furnishing them with food, but inadequate for war against the wild beasts—for men had not yet the political *techne*, of which a part is the *techne* of war—so they tried to assemble together and preserve themselves by founding cities. However, whenever they did assemble together, they used to *adikein* (wrong) each other, since they did not possess the political *techne*, with the result that their associations broke up and they continued to be

---

[1] It is customary to distinguish 'pre-Socratic philosophers', concerned with nature-philosophy, from sophists, concerned with rhetoric and politics. The distinction has some utility, but there is no lack of writers who were concerned with both cosmology and ethics or politics.

destroyed by wild beasts. Zeus, accordingly, in fear lest the whole human race should be destroyed, sent Hermes to bring to mortals *aidos* and *dike* (mutual respect and justice), in order that cities might have order and there might be bonds to hold together *philia* (human associations). Hermes asked Zeus how he was to give *dike* and *aidos* to mankind: 'Am I to allot them as the *technai* are allotted? They are allotted in this manner: one man possessing the *techne* of medicine suffices for many laymen, and similarly in the case of the other craftsmen. Am I thus to impart *dike* and *aidos* to mankind, or am I to allot them to all?' 'To all' said Zeus. 'Let all share in them; for cities would not come into being, if a few possessed them as is the case with the other *technai*; and make a *nomos* in my name that whoever is incapable of partaking in *aidos* and *dike* should be killed as a disease of the city.'

Here, despite the presence of the gods, justice is seen as essential to the existence of cities in an entirely naturalistic manner: injustice disrupts society.[1] The argument occurs in a justification of democracy; and the values are those which we might *a priori* expect a democracy to possess. Similarly, in Euripides (*Suppliant Women* 429 ff.), Theseus, constitutional ruler of Athens, says:

There is nothing more ill-disposed to a city than a tyrant, in that first of all there are no *nomoi* common to all, but one man holds sway, with the *nomos* in his own possession; and this is not *ison*, equal, fair. But when the *nomoi* are written down, the *asthenēs* (weak) and the wealthy have *isē* (equal) rights, and the more *asthenes* can, when he is abused, utter the same to him who is more *eutuchein* (fortunate), and the lesser can defeat the great if justice is on his side. This is *to eleutheron* (freedom): 'Who possesses some plan *chreston* (useful) to the city and wishes to bring it forward to public notice?' And he who wishes is famous, and he who does not wish, remains silent. What is more *ison* for a city than this?

What indeed! The laws are written down, common to all, and the weak can defeat the stronger in court if justice is on his side.

[1] Contrast e.g. Bacchylides 49, above p. 95.

Anyone who wishes, rich or poor, can express his views in the Assembly. Surely the disadvantages of Teucer are now removed?

The impression may be strengthened by a passage from Pericles' Funeral Speech (Thucydides II, 37):

> For we enjoy a form of government which does not emulate the *nomoi* of its neighbours; we rather serve as an example ourselves than imitate others. It is called democracy because we do not *oikein* in respect to a few, but to a greater number; and so far as the *nomoi* are concerned, all partake in *to ison* (equality) with respect to private disagreement, while so far as status is concerned one is advanced to public office not *apo merous* but rather from *arete*; but one is not prevented, if one is poor, by obscurity of status, at all events (*ge*) if one is able to *agathon drān* (benefit) the city.

Oikein here seems to be used of the extent of citizenship and its accompanying rights;[1] and that there is equality before the law is stated here too, with specific reference to the litigation of private individuals. The meaning of *apo merous* is disputed; but certainly *arete* is cited as the criterion for public office. What is commended by *arete* here must be discussed below: it is certainly stated in the following clauses that low social status does not prevent one from reaching a position of public prominence, *at all events* if one has anything to offer. 'At all events' will be considered further below:[2] the general impression, however, is certainly 'democratic'.

Thus far the *nomoi* concerned appear to be 'laws'; but, as is well known, *nomos* spans both 'law' and 'custom'. To try to establish the effect of this, it may be useful to quote a few examples where the creation of a *nomos* is mentioned.

In Euripides' *Electra* Orestes speaks of his acquittal on the charge of homicide at Athens when the votes were equal, and adds (1268):

> And for the future this *nomos* shall be *tithesthai* (established), that the defendant wins his case if the votes are equal.

[1] See A. W. Gomme, *A Historical Commentary on Thucydides*, vol. ii, pp. 108 f.
[2] See p. 141.

Evidently a law, or an aspect of a law; and it would be easy to cite parallels. However, in Euripides' *Suppliant Women* (537 ff.) Theseus asks the herald:

> Do you think that it is Argos that you are harming by not burying the dead? Not at all. All Greece is harmed if any-one is to keep the dead from what is their due, by denying them burial; for it engenders cowardice in the brave if this *nomos* is *tithesthai*.

Here there is evidently no question of a formally enacted law. Nor is this merely the speech of tragedy. In Thucydides (I, 40, 6) the Corinthians say to the Athenians:

> For if you are going to accept those who are doing some *kakon* and avenge them . . . you will *tithenai* a *nomos* which will be more to your disadvantage than to ours.

In these cases[1] what is *tithesthai*, established, is not a law, but rather a precedent, a precedent which the speaker holds likely to be followed. It must not be forgotten that the traditional society of Greece is very much custom-bound, and that where the one word *nomos* spans both law and custom, this fact may induce, and reflect, in the minds of the users of the language as high a regard for custom as for enacted law. Of course, once the different customs of different societies are noted, any re-sulting tendency to speak or think of 'mere custom' will effectively reduce the status of law, where both are *nomos*.

C. *Nomos* AND *Phusis*

In any case, failing a radical realignment of Greek values, the *nomos* must be held to be 'good for' one: it must be believed to be more profitable to be *nomos*-abiding than '*nomos*-less' if the *nomos* is to be respected. Earlier, in a traditional society, the threat of divine sanction might have been reinforced by respect for *nomos*, custom, law, tradition, *per se* in some cases;[2]

---

[1] Compare also Euripides, *Orestes* 564 ff., *Troades* 1029 ff. and Sophocles, *Electra* 577 ff.

[2] We have seen in writers from Homer onwards the inability of *moira* or *nomos* to withstand the demands of *arete* in a crisis; but only *agathoi* have *arete*, and one's *arete*, even if one has it, is not felt to be

but in the later fifth century everything was under scrutiny, and the shock-waves created by the impact of the sophistic movement must have been diffused widely through Greek society. In these circumstances, some, as we have seen, evidently believed that it paid to be law-abiding. Others did not, as Antiphon shows (Diels/Kranz B44):

Dikaiosune (justice), then, is not to transgress what is laid down by *nomos* in the city in which one lives. A man would accordingly make use of justice in a manner most advantageous to himself if he were to treat the *nomoi* as most important when witnesses were present, but the edicts of *phusis* (nature) as important when he is alone; for the edicts of the *nomoi* are adventitious, whereas those of *phusis* are necessary. Those of the *nomoi* arise out of compacts between men, not as a result of *phūnai* (natural growth), whereas those of *phusis* are a result of natural growth and do not arise out of compacts between men. Supposing, then, that a man transgresses what is laid down by *nomos*, if he escapes the notice of those who made the compact, he is free from both shame (*aischūnē*, linked with *aischron*) and actual damage, while if he does not escape notice, he does not escape those penalties; but supposing, against possibility, a man violates one of the requirements implanted by *phusis*, if he escapes the notice of all mankind, the damage to him is no less, and if all see, no more; for he is not damaged on account of an opinion, but on account of truth . . .

Now if those who submitted to the provisions (of the *nomoi*) received help, and those who did not, but opposed them, received damage, obeying the laws would not be without benefit; but as it is, *nomos* based on justice is not strong enough to help those who submit to such provisions . . .

The *nomoi* are not strong enough to be 'good for' one. (Yet the appearance of justice seems to pay, to judge from the

relevant in all situations. In a traditional society, when the demands of *arete* are not active *nomos* will be very powerful. Cf. Herodotus' anecdote about burial-customs (III, 38).

beginning of the quotation.) Further, there is something more important than *nomos*: *phusis*, usually translated 'nature', and here most evidently referring to the 'demands of nature'. If these are frustrated, real damage results: transgression of the *nomoi* merely brings down upon one the disapproval of one's fellows. (The argument is not fully thought out: 'against possibility' implies that it is impossible to act against *phusis*, whereas the beginning of the passage advises acting against *phusis* under certain circumstances, and the passage as a whole treats such behaviour as possible, even if inadvisable.) The words quoted incidentally destroy the argument of Critias' *Sisyphus*, if that passage is viewed as an inducement to be law- (or *nomos-*) abiding: if the harm that results from not following the behests of *phusis* is real, one will hardly be induced to follow *nomos* by dread of a god no longer held to be even a useful fiction, when one might be lawless by stealth.

The argument, as stated, is powerful; but in fact its power is even greater than is at first sight apparent, for *phusis*, as I have tried to show elsewhere,[1] is not adequately rendered by 'nature' and carries an emotive charge and associations which are concealed by any such translation.

If we are to appreciate the effects of the sophistic usage, we must also consider the history of the word *phusis* in 'ordinary Greek'. It is related—as indeed this very passage indicates—to *phunai*, 'grow', 'come to be'. In the earlier fifth century (where it is not a word at the centre of debate, and is used unself-consciously) it may be used to denote a human being's 'birth'; not simply the experience of being born, but one's high or low birth, together with all the material and social advantages or disadvantages that an individual derives from his being born into a particular station in society. It is not that *phusis* does not, in intention, advert to what is 'real' and innate; rather that the Greeks of the period unanalytically ascribed to 'birth' what we should distinguish as external as well as innate benefits. *Phusis*, then, traditionally denotes and—when the birth is high—commends 'birth and breeding' in ordinary Greek. In so doing, it reinforces the effect of traditional *arete*, which also tends to commend high birth (inasmuch as most

[1] *From the Many to the One*, pp. 79 ff.

agathoi were the children of *agathoi*), and of which external advantages form a considerable part. Traditionally, most *agathoi* were *agathoi* by birth, *phusis*, and their *arete* might be said to be theirs by *phusis* too.

This, however, is 'ordinary Greek'. By the later fifth century, medical writers and Presocratic philosophers were using *phusis* to denote what was 'real' in a much more analytic manner;[1] and the doctor least of all men has any inducement to ascribe to human *phusis* anything other than the physical and psychological constitution of his patient. Since it is reasonable to regard the sophists as living in the same intellectual climate as the scientific doctors and Presocratic philosophers, we might perhaps expect that, for the sophists and their pupils, *phusis* would denote only inherent human characteristics.

The matter, however, requires further study. The 'immoralist'[2] sophists and their pupils, as portrayed by Plato, give a different impression. In the *Gorgias* (483A7 ff.) Callicles says:

> According to *phusis*, everything is more *aischron* (shameful) which is also more *kakon* (harmful to oneself)—as, for example, suffering injustice; but according to *nomos* committing injustice is more *aischron*. For to suffer injustice is not an experience which befits a man, but one fit only for a slave for whom death is preferable to life; a man who when he is wronged or insulted is incapable of helping either himself or anyone else for whom he cares.

While in the *Republic* (344C) Thrasymachus declares that injustice is stronger, more 'liberal' and more befitting a master than justice.

We might perhaps have expected the sophists' view of *phusis* to be derived from nature-philosophy and medicine. When variations of *nomoi* are set on one side—and an increased knowledge of other cultures, such as became available in the fifth century, would assist in separating *nomos* from

---

[1] For evidence see *From the Many to the One*, pp. 91 ff.

[2] The word, frequently employed by modern writers to characterise Thrasymachus and Greeks holding similar views, is unjustified in terms of Greek values. See below, p. 119.

what is universal, and so perhaps arises from *phusis*—what remains is *phusis*, the basic drives, needs, 'nature' of man. There is indeed great emphasis on the satisfaction of the basic drives for food, drink and sex in such sophists and their pupils; but it seems doubtful whether their interpretation of human *phusis* could be derived wholly from medical sources. It may be possible to prescribe a way of life on the basis of even the first steps in medicine, as Democritus tries to do (Diels/Kranz, B3 and 191); but it is a way of life very different from that counselled by Antiphon and Callicles. None of the extant doctors deduces—or indeed was likely to deduce—from the fact that all men by *phusis* possess a stomach that *phusis* demands that one should at all times gratify the stomach to the utmost (as Callicles virtually counsels, Plato, *Gorgias* 494A6 ff.) and that it is better for the individual to do so. If we remember the traditional requirements of *arete*, however, the situation becomes clearer. *Agathos*, which always, as the most powerful term of value, commends 'the human being at his best', has traditionally commended a man endowed with material advantages by the circumstances of his birth, of whom it is expected that he will exert himself and succeed in securing and maintaining the well-being of the social unit, primarily household, secondarily city, with which he is associated. Should he succeed he is *agathos* and is manifesting *arete*. Now his ability to be *agathos* depends, at all periods discussed in this book, in most cases on the circumstances of his birth,[1] for most *agathoi* were the children of *agathoi*; and his birth may be spoken of as his *phusis*; so that the *agathos* child of an *agathos* family is *agathos* by *phusis*. Now *arete* had always enjoined upon the *agathos* that he should compete as successfully as possible and maximise his prosperity; and, his ability to do this depending on his birth, his *phusis*, in manifesting his *arete* he was also

---

[1] Sometimes, as in Theognis' Megara, the number of new *agathoi*—or would-be *agathoi*—seems to have been considerable; but the discussion of pp. 37 ff. shows the extreme reluctance of established *agathoi* to admit wealthy members of previously non-*agathoi* families to the circle of the *agathoi* (cf. also Cleon, pp. 139 ff.); and in most cities at most times the number of 'new rich' citizens cannot have been high.

manifesting his *phusis*. Accordingly, though in the *Gorgias* passage quoted above Callicles seems to be using the concept of *phusis* to determine what is *aischron*, and though the effectiveness of the idea of *phusis* must have been greatly enhanced by philosophical and medical thought and increased knowledge of the wide range of differing customs, *nomoi*, of other lands, it is nevertheless more accurate to say that the traditional idea of *arete* is serving to define the characteristics of *phusis* than that the concept of *phusis* is serving to define the characteristics of *arete*.

One might have expected the sophistic movement to have a powerful 'democratising' effect. The sophists professed a variety of skills; but most important, both in the society in which they flourished and in the present discussion, were the skills in rhetoric and administration, whether of household or city. Protagoras, in Plato's dialogue which bears his name, states (318E ff.):

> What they learn is *euboulia* (sound judgment) about their own affairs—how they may *arista dioikein* (best manage) their own households—and about the affairs of the city— how they may be most *dunatoi* (competent) to handle its business both in speech and action.

And he agrees when Socrates says:

> You seem to mean the *politikē techne* (political art), and to be promising to make men into *agathoi politai*.

While Gorgias in the *Gorgias*, though insisting (456C ff.) that the skill of rhetoric should be used justly, holds that it is (452D5 ff.)

> . . . in truth the greatest *agathon* and the cause both of *eleutheria* (freedom) for men themselves and of an individual's ruling over others in his city . . . I mean being able to persuade by one's words both jurymen in court and members of the Council in the Council and members of the Assembly in the Assembly and anyone in any kind of political gathering whatsoever. Through this power you will have the doctor and the trainer as your slaves; and the business man

will manifestly have been carrying on his business not for himself but for you who are able to speak and persuade the mass of the people.

Now there is a certain ambiguity in 'freedom for men themselves': Gorgias might be saying that the existence of orators in a state, and opportunities for them to speak, is an assurance that freedom will exist for all, that there will be no tyranny or close oligarchy. The words could, however, be read as 'freedom for individuals'; and whether they are so read or not, what follows, 'and (the cause) of an individual's ruling over others in the city . . . you will have the doctor and the trainer as your slaves . . .' shows once again that freedom, *eleutheria*, is in Greece a competitive combative concept, closely linked to *arete*, the quality which enables one to have freedom oneself and control over others.

Furthermore, though the sophists offered their skills 'to all', and 'the political skill' thus ceased to be handed down within families,[1] 'to all' does not imply that anyone with the necessary aptitude could obtain the best available training in rhetoric and 'the political art'. The full instruction offered by the sophists was expensive. As a result, the wealthy families of Athens were able to profit from such instruction, families who were already *agathoi* and who, by thus increasing their political effectiveness and power, acquired a new claim to be *agathoi*, and *agathoi politai*, 'good citizens', a phrase whose implications require careful study. It should not be hastily assumed that being an *agathos polites* demands just co-operation with one's fellow citizens. It certainly explicitly links the *agathos* with the *polis*; but there are other links than just co-operation. This one quotation, indeed, indicates that being an *agathos polites* may be thought of as a skill: later discussion will indicate whether or no that skill need be exercised justly.

D. NEW VALUES

I have already quoted some passages which seem to be 'democratic' in tone. We must now consider whether *arete*, and the

[1] In (ironic) deference to tradition, Socrates suggests in the doubtfully Platonic *Theages* (126C ff.) (and cf. *Protagoras* 319E) that

other most powerful value-terms of the society, were redefined in use in a manner which reflected such 'democratic' aspirations. Callicles' words from the *Gorgias*, and other material already discussed, indicate that at least some Greeks continued to use *arete* and allied words to commend successful competition; but we have yet to try to estimate the extent to which these are unusual in the later fifth century. Callicles and Thrasymachus are frequently termed 'immoralists': what is meant by this, and is it true?

First some examples of 'new values', in which words from the *arete*-group are used to commend behaviour in accordance with co-operative excellences, or to decry breaches of co-operative excellences. The latter, at least, is found already in Aeschylus. In the *Suppliant Women* (402 ff.) the Chorus says

> Zeus . . . watches over these things, and holds the balance, assigning to the *kakoi* their *adika* (unjust deeds), to the *ennomoi* (law-abiding) their *hosia* (righteous deeds).

Being *kakos* is here linked with injustice and opposed to being law-abiding and righteous; and thus being *kakos* is associated with the breach of (at least some) co-operative excellences. Similar usages are found in Sophocles (*Ajax* 132 f.); and in Euripides the usage is frequent and quite unrestricted. (In Aeschylus it is confined to generalisations, and does little to affect his usage of value-terms in other respects.)

Aischron, the most powerful word available to decry an action, behaves similarly. Aeschylus' usage seems to show that he felt some difficulty in using it to decry breaches of co-operative excellences,[1] though Io holds it to be *aischron* to tell lies (*Prometheus Bound* 685 f.). In the context, no success would be achieved by telling the lie: there is no conflict between the

---

Demodocus should take his son (127A) to one of 'the *kaloi kagathoi* in respect of politics' in order to have him trained as a politician. ('*Kaloi kagathoi*' suggests that the upper classes are held to be the repository of political skill.)

[1] See *Agamemnon* 222, 401, and the discussion in *Merit and Responsibility* 181 f.

kalon of success and the *aischron* of lying. Similarly, Pindar can adjure Hiero (*Pythians* I, 85):

> Nevertheless, since to be envied is better than to be pitied, do not disregard actions which are *kala*: govern your people with a just helm, and hammer out your speech on a truthful anvil.

Here, truth-telling is *kalon*, as lying or suppressing the truth was *aischron* in Aeschylus. But it also seems to be *kalon* to be just; and this is an advance. Note that the justice concerned, however, is that of the superior who has jurisdiction over inferiors, not that of equals before the law. The distinction is important: to secure justice with one's strong right arm for one's dependants, or for others, as Heracles did in some of his labours, is traditionally the work of the *agathos*: Heracles is the paradigm of traditional *arete*. It might well be easier to extend *kalon* to commend the peaceful dispensing of justice by one in power—though, it should be emphasised, even this is a new development in the earlier fifth century—than to use it to commend the co-operation of equal citizens. Heracles would have been a disturbing next-door neighbour.

In none of these passages is any conflict presented between 'traditional' and 'new' *arete*. For this, we must consider authors later in the century. In Euripides' *Phoenician Women* the blind Oedipus, to dissuade Antigone from her expressed intention to accompany him in exile, says (1691 f.):

> For a daughter to be exiled with her blind father is *aischron*.

He receives the reply,

> It is not *aischron* but *gennaion* (noble), at all events if she *sophronein* (is a virtuous woman).

Here the denial that wandering poverty with the disgraced, blinded, polluted Oedipus, is *aischron* flies in the face of traditional *arete*: the conflict is evident. Similarly, in Sophocles' *Philoctetes* (1234, 1248), Neoptolemus insists on returning the bow he has obtained from Philoctetes by trickery on the grounds that he obtained it *aischrōs* and unjustly, and that he has committed a *hamartiā aischrā*, a shameful 'error', by so doing. Here *aischron* is used to decry an action which has succeeded in depriving Philoctetes of the magic bow, a desired end which will lead to the much more desired end of capturing Troy: a violent collision with traditional values.

Examples in the earlier fifth century are, as we should perhaps already expect, very scanty; but Euripides and the later plays of Sophocles seem to indicate that the change in values is now complete. However, we have not yet considered *agathos* and *arete*; and it must be remembered that injustice may render an *agathos*—endowed with all the traditional advantages—*kakos* without justice rendering a poor *kakos agathos*: justice may be a necessary, but not sufficient, condition of *arete*. It must also be remembered that we have not yet discussed the frequency of this usage as compared with persisting 'traditional' usages.

First, the use of *agathos* and *arete* to commend just behaviour in a man. There are no examples in Aeschylus or Sophocles, and the one example of *agathos* so used in the extant complete plays of Euripides is illuminating. Orestes has just discovered that the Husbandman has not attempted to consummate his marriage with Electra, given to him by Aegisthus on the grounds that such a husband, and any children they might have, would be little danger to his usurped throne. Orestes is amazed and (*Electra* 367 ff.) begins to reflect upon *euandriā*, the condition of the *agathos* man: a type of word which, as is to be expected, traditionally denotes and commends courage and the social attributes of the *agathos*. Now, however, Orestes is puzzled: *phusis*, he says, is variable from one generation to another,[1] and a *gennaios*, noble, father may have a useless offspring and *vice versa*. Birth, then, is not a satisfactory criterion of *arete*; and Orestes quickly rejects the claims of wealth also. But poverty is not a mark of the *agathos* either: 'poverty is a diseased condition and teaches a man to do *kakon*, harm, by reason of need.' Greeks of this period did not regard poverty as an *arete*, or as a concomitant of *arete*: the conditions of life in a Greek city made such a judgment

[1] Euripides is here challenging traditional assumptions about *phusis*, for which see *From the Many to the One*, pp. 79 ff.

virtually impossible. Orestes next rejects weapons as a criterion of one's *arete* (the cavalry and hoplite-classes being tradition-ally the *agathoi*): one cannot tell who is *agathos* merely by looking at his weapons. (In the context of Greek values even this point must have been difficult to understand.) Orestes has been shocked into questioning traditional assumptions:

> For this man, who neither has a high position among the Argives, nor is puffed up by the fame deriving from noble lineage, but is a man of the people, has proved to be *aristos*. Will you not come to your senses,[1] you who wander about full of empty opinion, and in future judge men by their mode of life, and determine who is *eugenēs* (noble) by his mode of behaviour?

This is a powerful appeal, whose vehemence is perhaps explained by the fact that it seems to be not only the assump-tions and linguistic behaviour of the audience that Euripides is trying to change, but his own. The Husbandman is here—apparently—commended as *aristos*, most *agathos*, for his self-control; but nowhere else in the extant complete plays of Euripides is any male character commended as *agathos* for self-control or for any co-operative excellence. In general, the usage is rare, even in the later fifth century. In Herodotus—who uses 'co-operative' *kakos* and *kakotes* quite freely—there is only one example, in a highly 'sophistic' context.[2] One passage of Thucydides goes even further. When the Cor-cyreans requested an alliance from the Athenians in the Athenian Assembly, the Corinthians in reply said of them (I, 37, 5):

> If they were *agathoi*, as they claim to be, the less they could be assailed by their neighbours, the more clearly could they have displayed their *arete* by giving and receiving what was just, *dikaion*.

Thucydides, an intellectual writer aware of all the intel-lectual currents of his day, here indicates that to be *agathos*, to

[1] This is evidently the sense, though the Greek is obscure; see J. D. Denniston, Euripides, *Electra*, Oxford 1939, ad loc.
[2] III, 80. See *Merit and Responsibility* p. 178.

display *arete*, may now be to observe without compulsion the claims of *dikaiosune* even in relations between states: an even more striking novelty than the *arete* of quiet just behaviour towards one's fellow-citizens.

There are, however, few examples of the usage, even in the later fifth century, and in writers who reflect the 'New Thought'. Traditional *arete* still holds its own; and the reason will soon become apparent. How was anyone to be convinced that the new *arete* was indeed an *arete*? One might take the 'gentlemanly' overtones of traditional *arete*, and claim that it was 'gentlemanly' to be just; and this seems to have been attempted.[1] If, however, this did not suffice, some further proof must be tried; and if we continue the quotation from the *Electra*, the kind of proof offered will become apparent. Thus far, the Husbandman seems to be commended purely for his self-control; but Orestes immediately adds (386 ff.):

> For such men *eu oikein* (administer well) both their cities and their own households, whereas those who are nothing but senseless lumps of muscle are mere ornaments of the market-place, for a strong arm does not even endure a spear-thrust any better than a weak one. No; such ability lies in a man's *phusis* and in his *eupsūchiā* (excellence of spirit).

Self-control renders a man *agathos* because men who are self-controlled are good at administering both their cities and their own households. Such good administration was what Protagoras, quoted above, and other sophists professed to teach; and it constituted the political art, and rendered men *agathoi politai*. It should be apparent from previous chapters, and will soon be further demonstrated in this chapter, that in this situation the success resulting from the administration is the valued goal, to which all else is a means. If self-control is acknowledged to be a necessary means, it will be valued;[2] but if it, or anything else, appears ineffective, then it will be rejected in favour of what appears more effective; and this is commended by the

[1] See *Merit and Responsibility* chapter ix, and for fourth-century writers chapter xvi, pp. 336 ff.

[2] Cf. Plato, *Meno* 71 E ff., p. 133 below, and *Merit and Responsibility* pp. 228 ff.

traditional pattern and balance of Greek values. Success is the goal; and any moderation in its pursuit has been enjoined upon the outstanding individual by the belief that the gods would allow more success to the moderate than to the man of excess. If the belief was not held, moderation could not be effectively commended. Some Greeks have now ceased to believe in gods altogether,[1] and a secular commendation of the quieter excellences is needed. Such commendation can only be effective if the quieter excellences are acknowledged to contribute to the success and prosperity of the household and city—and to contribute more than would qualities that conflict and are incompatible with these. The question is empirical, and a question rather of political theory than of ethics; and no answer is ruled out. If a Thrasymachus supposes, and believes that he can demonstrate, that injustice, *adikia*, is more profitable than justice, then Greek values justify his terming *adikia* an *arete*; as he of course realises (*Republic* 348C ff.):

SOCRATES: Do you term *dikaiosune arete*, and *adikia*, *kakia*?

THRASYMACHUS: That's *very* likely, my amusing friend, when I say that *adikia* is profitable and *dikaiosune* not profitable!

Thrasymachus naturally regards *adikia* as an *arete*, and though he cannot quite bring himself to term *dikaiosune* a *kakia*—it has traditionally been neither an *arete* nor a *kakia*—he stigmatises it as 'a truly noble simplicity', the word translated 'simplicity' having the literal sense of 'good nature', but being used to decry the type of person who is too stupid to come in out of the rain. He treats the unjust as practically intelligent, *phronimoi*, 348D:

Those, at least, who are able to be completely unjust, and subject whole cities and races to themselves.

Petty crime is profitable, and so choiceworthy; but it is not worth consideration in comparison with the large-scale in-

[1] Some merely do not believe that the gods punish the wrongdoer; but the speaker in Critias' *Sisyphus*-fragment (above, p. 102) believes that the gods are fictions.

justice of the man, or small group, who can gain political power in their own interests.

Thrasymachus has already (344C) stated his belief that *adikia* is more powerful, more befitting a free man (*eleutherios*) and a master (*despotikos*) than justice. Since *arete* commends the qualities which enable a man to be free himself and rule over and control others, *adikia* is once again commended as an *arete*; which is to say that it is commended as powerfully as possible.

Thrasymachus and his like are frequently termed 'immoralists'; but this is surely misleading. They are immoralists from our point of view, for we, as a society, at least declare our acceptance of basic values of which Thrasymachus' words are a rejection; but Thrasymachus is merely drawing out what appear to him to be the logical consequences of Greek values, using as one premiss what he takes to be the fundamental fact of the situation: that injustice *is* more profitable than justice, provided it can obtain free rein. He can be refuted only by demonstrating that justice is in fact the more profitable; as Plato seeks to do in the *Republic*. Nor is this true only of Thrasymachus and his like: all Greeks need to be convinced that the co-operative excellences are profitable before they will pursue them, and value most highly, as *aretai*, those qualities which appear to contribute most to the goals which they propose, and traditionally have proposed, to themselves. In the remainder of this chapter I shall examine the effects of these values in different areas of Athenian life.

E. THE COURTS OF DEMOCRATIC ATHENS

In the later fifth century, Athens was a democracy. We are told as much by the Athenians of the period, so we presumably cannot doubt it. Certainly the city had very democratic institutions; democratic to such an extent that we might perhaps expect that the *agathoi* had a hard time of it, or even that the mass of the citizens would take over the terms *agathos* and *arete* and apply them to themselves, as the most valuable members of the city. After all, the poorer citizens furnished the oarsmen of the fleet, on which, far more than the hoplites, the well-being of Athens' empire depended, as was realised. Observers such as the 'Old Oligarch' acknowledge the importance of the navy as the justification for Athens' increasedly democratic institutions (Pseudo-Xenophon, *Constitution of Athens*, 1, 2). However, though the 'Old Oligarch' recognises and admits this truth, we should never forget that the document was written by a traditional *agathos* with an eye jaundiced and disposed to exaggerate when faced with any aspirations of those who were traditionally *kakoi*. If we accept his highly emotive language as simple description, we may conclude that in all matters the poorer Athenian was now wont to assert that his importance and status was equal with that of the wealthiest *agathos*. We should be wary: much evidence points in the opposite direction.

The courts of democratic Athens appear to be one of her most democratic institutions. Membership of the juries, which might contain as many as 501 persons, was open to all; and, with the institution of pay for dicasts by Pericles about 450, became—as it was intended to do—a valuable financial relief for the poorer citizens. Even had they wished, the wealthy could hardly have guaranteed themselves a majority on any jury at any time, and would certainly have been in a minority on most juries at most times; but in addition the association of jury-service with poor-relief, which must have given it a social stigma in the eyes of the *agathos*, and the small inducement the wealthier citizen had to sit on a jury, must have further reduced the proportion of *agathoi* likely to be present at any time when a case was tried. Now Aristotle (*Constitution of Athens*, 9) says that 'when the common people gains control of the jury-vote, it gains control of the constitution'; and the former the common people of Athens undeniably possessed. Again, they constituted large assemblies of amateurs who were at once juries and judges, and received no professional advice, for the Greek court had no professional judges or lawyers. Unless the Athenian juror was more self-controlled than Greek values as they have appeared so far give us reason to expect, surely the *agathos* tried in such a court is likely to have been at a great disadvantage. True, the jurors swore an oath to vote in accordance with the laws, and the decrees of the Assembly and Council; in matters not covered by laws or decrees, to

120

decide impartially, without favour or enmity; to favour neither the accusers nor the defendants; and to consider only the facts of the case (Demosthenes 24, 149 ff.). But with no professional advice, surely the prejudices of the common people in favour of their own kind are bound to creep in. Euripides (*Suppliant Women*, 429 ff.) has already informed us[1] that where there are written laws the weak and the wealthy are equal before the law: in these circumstances, we might suppose that the advantages of the weak, that is, the poor, are underestimated.

After such *a priori* generalities it is surprising to discover the pleas actually offered in Athenian courts of law. In Lysias' twenty-fifth speech, the defendant[2] is rebutting a charge of having subverted the democracy: it was evidently plausible— to put it no more strongly—that he had oligarchic sympathies. He endeavours to show that he has never actively support-ed oligarchy; but in his defence he includes the following (12):

> I was trierarch five times; I fought in a sea battle four times; I made many contributions of money to the public finances; and I performed the other 'liturgies' in a manner not inferior to any other citizen. And I spent more money on these than I was required to do by the city, so that I might be thought more *agathos* by you, and if some misfortune should come upon me, I might *ameinon agōnizesthai* (fare better in court).

Now this speaker is also protesting his innocence; but openly to avow that one has spent money in order to be thought more *agathos* and have a better chance in court if put on trial must appear to us to fly in the face of the justice that the jury swore to observe. Yet Lysias was a skilled speech-writer: he must have known what would sway the jury.

There are considerations that may be set against strict justice even when, as is not the case in the passage discussed above,

[1] Above, p. 104.

[2] In Athens a prosecutor or defendant had to conduct his own case; but he might employ a professional to compose his speech for him. Lysias is usually writing speeches to be delivered by others.

that justice is mentioned. In Lysias' thirtieth speech, the speaker begins

> Gentlemen of the jury, there have been people who when put on trial appeared to *adikein* (be guilty), but who, when they declared the *aretai* of their ancestors and their own benefits (to the city) received *sungnōmē* (pardon) at your hands.

Later in the speech, the speaker enquires (26)

> What reason could one have for acquitting this man? That he has been an *agathos* against our enemies and has been present at many battles on land and sea? But while you were sailing out on dangerous expeditions, he stayed at home and corrupted the laws of Solon. That he has spent money (on the city) and made many contributions to public finances? But not only has he not given you any of his own property, he has embezzled a great deal of your (i.e. public) property. Because of his ancestors? For some have in the past obtained pardon from you for this reason. But this man deserves to die on his own account, and on his ancestors'—to be sold. Or is the reason to be that, if you spare him now, he will repay your favours later? But he does not even remember the *agatha* (benefits) that he received from you before.

The speaker does not claim that any of these pleas should be regarded as invalid in court: he simply asserts that the present defendant—alleged to be an ex-slave and an embezzler—is in no position to benefit from them. Certain aspects of the speech imply that the speaker has oligarchic tendencies, while the accused is a servant of the democracy of long standing; yet this attack can be made, presumably—since it is made—with good hope of success.

Emotional pleas for pity were notoriously sometimes made in Athenian courts; but these speakers seem not to be asking for pity, but rather for admiration for qualities which we should not regard as relevant in court, but which are apparently not debarred from the Athenian court even by the oath to decide on the merits of the case. At all events, the speaker in Lysias' third speech says (46 ff.):

> I could say many other things about him, but since it is not *nomimon* (lawful, customary) in your court to speak of matters outside the case in hand, consider this: these are the men who entered our house by force, these who pursued us, these who dragged us out of our path by force. Remember this and vote *ta dikaia* (what is just), and do not overlook the fact that I am being *adikōs* (unjustly) expelled from my country, for which I have endured many dangers and performed many 'liturgies', and have never caused it any *kakon* (harm), neither I nor any of my relatives, but rather many *agatha* (benefits).

If we took seriously the speaker's resolve not to introduce material irrelevant to the case, it would appear that his own merits are not irrelevant, though mention of other crimes committed by his opponent would be. This would be a hazardous inference, and certainly speakers do deliver general attacks on the character and behaviour of their opponents; but possibly we might conclude that the closeness of the mention of irrelevance and that of the speaker's 'liturgies' gives grounds for supposing that the jury was not predisposed to regard the latter as irrelevant.

There are, indeed, strong arguments for supposing the contrary. For what are these pleas supposed to establish? 'Liturgies' are public services performed by the contribution of sums of money: for commissioning a trireme, for furnishing a comic, tragic, or dithyrambic chorus, and for other purposes. They are expensive, and can only be performed by substantial citizens. And here the theory that it is the *agathos* who is at a disadvantage in the Athenian courts founders on the facts of Greek economic life. The poorer citizens certainly were the basis of Athens' naval power; as they were able to be since, unlike the hoplites, they did not provide their own weapons. As has been said, this situation encouraged democratic aspirations; but the state provided only the hulls and tackle of the triremes, the Greek warships of the day. The ships were maintained and repaired by private individuals, wealthy individuals: not as contributors to some general tax pool, but as the identifiable furnishers of the needs of a specific ship (as, in the case of other 'liturgies', they were the identifiable providers of a particular chorus). Without 'liturgies' there would have been no Athenian navy, and no Empire; the performers of 'liturgies' were known, and the contribution of each to the well-being of Athens was manifestly greater than that of any individual oarsman. Furthermore, they belonged to the class that were traditionally *agathoi* in virtue of their contribution to the well-being of the state; and by referring to their 'liturgies', contributions of money and other public services, their own and their ancestors', they are, as the speakers in Lysias make clear, claiming to be *agathoi* or *agathoi politai*. To be *agathos* had always been more important than merely to be *dikaios*, and one's injustice did not traditionally—nor, it is clear, in the Athenian courts—impair one's *arete*. Again, to be *agathos* was to be a specimen of the human being at his best, making to society the contribution that society valued most; and the poorer citizens could not deny this, nor yet that they were not *agathoi* themselves. In accepting *arete* as more important than *dikaiosune* they were of course not letting their hearts run away with their heads, but treating the well-being of the city as more important than the injustice of an individual: a calculation of advantages. Speakers (as in Lysias 21, 12, Aeschines, *Against Ctesiphon* 8) repeatedly urge the juries to vote for them by saying that their case is both just, *dikaion*, and advantageous, *agathon*, *lusiteloun* or *sumpheron*, to the city. In fact, these large juries, without professional advice, function virtually as sub-committees of the Assembly and accept arguments which we should regard as more appropriate to the political arena than to the law-courts.[1]

These values, as Greek values have always done, furnish the most powerful inducement to the *kakos* to show deference to the *agathos*, the poor specimen of human being to the human

[1] Cf. Cleon, Thucydides III, 40, 4, below, p. 134. Whether in court or in the Assembly, one may of course claim that one's proposal is just in addition to claiming that it is advantageous; but a survey of the extant documents can leave in no doubt which consideration had the greater weight.

being at his best. In Lysias' twelfth speech the speaker, here Lysias himself, says (38):

> Now he is not in a position to do what is so customary in this city—to make no defence to the accusation, and say other things by means of which they sometimes deceive you, representing to you that they are *agathoi* soldiers, or that as trierarchs they have captured many enemy ships, or have made friendly to us cities that previously were hostile. Tell him to show us where they killed as many of our enemies as of our citizens, or took as many ships as they themselves handed over to the enemy, or what city they brought over to our side so great as yours, which they enslaved. . . .

Lysias is prosecuting Eratosthenes for killing Lysias' brother Polemarchus. He has no difficulty in establishing the facts; and Eratosthenes was one of the Thirty Tyrants, the small group of extreme and violent oligarchs who had conducted a Reign of Terror in Athens at the end of the Peloponnesian War. It might appear *prima facie*—without considering Athenian values —that Eratosthenes at this time would have had no chance of acquittal even had he been innocent, in the light of his general political behaviour, which must have been abhorrent to any democrat. Yet Lysias finds it necessary to rebut this possible plea; Eratosthenes, an extreme oligarch, wealthy, an *agathos*, could doubtless have produced an impressive list of 'liturgies' to establish his *arete*; and Lysias fears that even in this extreme case *arete* is likely to prevail. Accordingly, he opposes to the 'liturgies', undeniably *agatha* to the city in themselves, much greater *kaka* that Eratosthenes has inflicted on the city. 'Sometimes deceive you' is not a rejection of the relevance of such *agatha* in court: Lysias does not say 'the injustice of the defendant is more important than his *arete*': he is arguing that such *agatha* will not serve to acquit Eratosthenes since in his case they are counterbalanced by more numerous *kaka of the same kind*, which show him not to be an *agathos* or *agathos polites*; and this is surely an index of the deference that the *kakos* felt for the *agathos*.

At all times in ancient Greece the views of all but *agathoi* have to be inferred; for only *agathoi* wrote books, and so only

125

the views of a sub-class of the *agathoi* have come down to us. However, when anyone is making a speech in the hope of persuading an audience of non-*agathoi*, and when many speakers use similar modes of persuasion, it is surely reasonable to suppose that the values and modes of argument employed are acceptable to the audience, particularly when powerful reasons can be found for their accepting them. On the other side, of course, we must set the complaints about the activities of sycophants in the later fifth century. The word is difficult to define:[1] its emotive charge is powerful, its descriptive meaning vague. It is used to decry false accusers, but seems to be available to decry any behaviour that the writer regards as scoundrelly in a legal context. Now doubtless the freedom, enjoyed by all Athenian citizens since the time of Solon, to prosecute wrongdoers was sometimes abused; and certainly wealthy *agathoi* offered the most attractive targets, for the financial rewards to the successful accuser might be very high in such cases. But we must remember that *agathoi* express all the complaints we have about sycophants; and the number of defendants who admit that they are guilty of serious offences is never very large. Xenophon says that the Thirty began by killing those 'who lived by being sycophants and were *barus*, a nuisance, to the *kaloi kagathoi*' (*Hellenica* II. iii. 12). Being *barus* to the *kaloi kagathoi*, the 'gentlemen' of Athens, might well be a sufficient condition for being regarded by them as a sycophant, and thus decried as a false and scoundrelly accuser. The latter presumably existed: the rewards that were offered could hardly have failed to attract rogues; but we should not take our sources at face value; and the extant forensic speeches indicate that, if accused, whether by a false or a justified accuser, the *agathos* was in a strong position.

F. *Arete* WITHIN THE CITY

Thus far, then, the *agathos polites* appears as someone who has conferred a benefit on his city; the valued benefits are material, and can only be conferred by the wealthier citizens; and when the *agathos* has conferred such benefits, the courts seem likely

[1] See Bonner and Smith, *The Administration of Justice from Homer to Aristotle*, Chicago 1938, vol. ii, p. 42.

to approve his *arete* rather than condemn his *adikia*. But the *agathos polites* has other aspects: as we have seen, the sophists taught the young—for the most part the wealthy young—the 'political art', or how to be *agathoi politai*; and this art is, as Protagoras said in Plato's dialogue, *euboulia*, skilful planning, in the field of their own affairs, so that they can competently manage both their own households and the city, in speech and in action. To show oneself to be an *agathos polites* by spending one's own money on public enterprises is, of course, to confer a generous favour on the city, for which one expects—for example, in court—benefits in return; the other aspects of *arete* exerted in public life, however, are attractive to oneself; and we must now consider the relationship of these aspects to the co-operative excellences.

There may, of course, be goals within the society with which its values are incompatible. There has long been a desire for civic stability; and also for that success in war without which the city, if attacked, might well cease to exist. *Arete* has traditionally commended the qualities conducive to success in war; and is still widely so used in the later fifth century. However, by this time, in some parts of society, even if the results are not apparent in the law-courts, thought and analysis are being devoted to the question of the types of behaviour most likely to avert civic strife, *stasis*.

In Sophocles' *Antigone* (658 ff.) Creon says of Antigone:

So let her call on Zeus of kindred blood; for if I am to rear those who are my kin by *phusis* to be disobedient, certainly I must bear with it in those outside the family. For whoever is *chrestos* (synonym for *agathos*) among the members of his family will be found to be *dikaios* in the city also. I should be confident that this man would rule *kalōs*, and be willing to *archesthai eu* (be a good subject), and would remain at his post in the storm of spears, a *dikaios* and *agathos* comrade. But whoever transgresses and either does violence to the *nomoi* or thinks to give orders to those in power—he can never gain praise from me. No; one must obey whomsoever the city may appoint in small matters and in great, in just matters and in unjust. There is no greater *kakon*

127

(harm) than *anarchiā*. This it is that destroys cities, this it is that overturns *oikoi*; this causes routs in battle; but of those who prosper, *peitharchiā* (obedience) saves the greater part.

Compare Archidamus, King of Sparta, discussing Spartan character and institutions (Thucydides I, 84, 3):

> We became warlike and *eubouloi* (able to manage our affairs to our own advantage[1]) as a result of our orderly behaviour; warlike, because *aidos* (a proper sense of shame) partakes most largely of *sophrosune*, and *eupsuchia* (courage) of *aischune* (here apparently synonymous with *aidos*); and *eubouloi* by being educated in such a manner as to be too ignorant to despise the *nomoi*, and through harsh treatment too *sophron* to disobey them.

Thirdly, Cleon, in the speech on the Mytileneans already discussed in part, says, to dissuade the Athenians from changing the resolution passed at the earlier assembly (Thucydides III, 37, 3 ff.):

> And it will be most terrible of all if nothing of what you resolve here is to remain firm and unchanged, and you are not going to take the view that a city which has *nomoi* that are more *kakoi* and leaves them undisturbed is *kreissōn* (stronger, more *agathos*) than one where the laws *kalōs echein* (are good) but have no authority, and that *amathiā* (ignorance) combined with *sophrosune* is more beneficial than *dexiotēs* (cleverness) combined with licence, and that the more *phauloi* (synonym for *kakoi*) of mankind for the most part *ameinon oikein* (more successfully govern) cities than do the more *sunetoi* (intelligent). For the latter wish to appear more *sophoi* (clever) than the *nomoi*, and to get the best of it whenever speeches are made in the assembly, on the grounds that there are no more important occasions on which they can display their views; and they for the most part cause cities disasters by such means, whereas those who distrust their own *sunesis* (intelligence) and hold themselves to be

[1] I suggest this translation to emphasise the importance of results: 'of good counsel' commends success, even if ignorance is a necessary ingredient of one's *euboulia*; as Archidamus holds it to be.

more ignorant than the *nomoi*, and less capable of finding
fault with the speech of him who speaks *kalōs*, but are
judges on equal terms rather than *agōnistai* (contenders)—
they for the most part prosper. Accordingly we (the orators)
should act in this manner and not, elated by our cleverness
and by a contest of *sunesis*, advise you, the mass of the
people, against our (your?) true opinion.

We have here three passages, none very closely related to
its context, and all abounding in generalisations. There are
differences: Creon is attempting to deduce a necessity for
discipline in peace from its necessity, particularly evident in a
hoplite-phalanx, in war, while Archidamus seems to distinguish the conditions for becoming warlike and for becoming
eubouloi; and the necessity of not being clever appears only in
Archidamus and Cleon. However, the passages have strong
resemblances; and appear to present a set of beliefs widely
current in the later fifth century. Obedience is at a premium,
the *nomoi* should be supreme even when they are inferior
nomoi, and ignorant acquiescence in their commands is better
—better for the city, more conducive to its prosperity and
stability—than cleverness. The words are put into the mouth
of Creon, a stage tyrant; Archidamus, a Spartan King; and
Cleon, an Athenian demagogue. Their only common characteristic is that they are in positions of authority: the view can
be ascribed to very different people.

It is evidently a view conducive to the harmonious function-
ing of cities, and also convenient for the ruler or rulers. We
must next enquire how it accords with traditional *arete*. Creon
maintains that the governed should obey in all things, whether
just or unjust; and this resembles other passages. Solon is said
(Diogenian *Proverbs* ii, 99) to have expressed the same view;
but a verse cited by the scholiast on Aeschylus, *Prometheus
Bound* 75[1] has 'Slave, obey your masters in matters just and
unjust'; and another proverb has 'One must obey those who
are *kreissones*, stronger, more *agathoi*, in matters just and unjust.' It is the mark of the weaker, the *kakos*, pre-eminently
the mark of the slave, so to submit: the mark of the *agathos*,

[1] See Jebb, *Antigone*, Cambridge 1888, note on 666 f.

the *eleutheros*, the free man, to do the opposite. Furthermore, Archidamus and Cleon hold that it is better to be stupid, which is certainly a mark of *kakia*, not of *arete*; and Cleon even uses *phaulos*, virtually a synonym for *kakos*, of those who *oikein* cities more successfully.

In the interests of civic well-being, then, citizens are being urged to be *kakoi*; and certainly it had been realised by some that traditional *arete* was a disruptive influence in cities. Darius in Herodotus III, 82—part of a sophistic debate on the best kind of constitution, transposed by Herodotus to Persia— says, in criticism of oligarchy and praise of monarchy:

> In an oligarchy, when many are exercising their *arete* in public affairs, powerful private *echthĕă* (enmities) are wont to develop; for since each man wishes to be leader himself, and to have his views *nikan* (prevail), they form powerful *echthea* against each other, from which civic strife develops. . . .

Traditional *arete* has the same effects in an oligarchy and in a democracy; and Cleon holds that a city is better without it. But *arete* commends the most highly valued qualities, those held to be most necessary to the well-being of the city; and if obedience is most necessary, obedience should be the most important *arete*. In the *Laws*, Plato ranks courage as the fourth grade of *arete* (667A), and says (922A):

> The greatest honour is to be given to those who are able to observe to an outstanding degree the written pronouncement of their good legislators.

Obedience to law thus, at the end of Plato's life, is ranked as the most important *arete*; but such a re-ranking is beyond the abilities of the later fifth century; and certainly no-one will obey when obedience is correlated with being *phaulos*, *kakos* and stupid, if *arete* is open to him.

When the speakers in the Assembly vie with one another in their speeches, they are trying to show themselves severally more effective than each other in directing and transacting the city's affairs, by persuading the assembly to vote for their proposals; and to do this successfully is a mark of *arete*, as we see both from Herodotus III, 82, and from the words of the sophists and rhetoricians (above, pp. 111 ff.) who attempted to teach the appropriate skills to would-be politicians. While such activity is denoted and commended by *arete*, as an activity of the utmost importance, an activity by which one shows oneself to be *kakos* has little chance of proving attractive, even if the city is the primary object of one's loyalty. Again, the question whether or no obedience to the laws conduces to civic stability under all circumstances is an experimental issue, on which different views were doubtless held by different Greeks who considered the matter—not necessarily a very large number—at this period; whereas anything commended as an *arete* is desirable *per se*.

Furthermore, the city was not the primary object of loyalty. Meno, portrayed as an 'ordinary *agathos*'[1] by Plato, says, *Meno* 71E 2 ff.:

> If you want a definition of the *arete* of a man, that is easy enough: the *arete* of a man is to be capable of taking an active part in politics, and while doing so, to be capable of helping one's *philoi* (friends) and harming one's *echthroi* (enemies within the city), while taking care to suffer no harm oneself at their hands.

This is Meno's first definition of *arete*; of which he also says, 73C9, 'What else is it than the capacity for ruling men?'; while at 77B4 it is 'to desire what is *kalon* and be able to obtain it'; and at 78C1, 'the power to obtain the *agatha*'.

[1] 'Ordinary *agathos*' may appear surprising, in view of *Anabasis* II, 6, 21 ff., where Xenophon portrays Meno as a greedy and treacherous scoundrel, who preyed on his friends because they were less likely to be on their guard against him than were his enemies. This may be historically accurate; but Plato paints a quite different portrait. Meno's views should be compared with those of Crito (Plato, *Crito* 45C5 ff.). He seems to set a higher value on the co-operative excellences than does the decent Athenian paterfamilias Crito. (I discuss this question in *Merit and Responsibility* 230 ff., and give my reasons for supposing that the values of Plato's Crito and Meno in fact closely resemble each other, and are characteristic of the *agathos* of the day.) Plato is not on oath when he is writing. (Nor is Xenophon.)

For the 'ordinary Greek', *arete* denotes and commends the capacity to obtain successes and benefits for one's *philoi*, a group smaller than the city—in the case of anyone active in politics, a political faction: *philos* denotes those who belong to the group or groups with whom one co-operates. An earlier passage of Meno's discussion with Socrates (73A6 ff.) will further illuminate the concept of *arete*:

SOCRATES: Were you not saying that the *arete* of a man is to *eu dioikein* (administer well) his city, the *arete* of a woman to do the same for her household?

MENO: Yes.

SOCRATES: Well, is it possible to administer anything *eu* (well)—city or household or anything else whatever—if one does not do it *sophronōs* and *dikaiōs* (in a 'prudent' and just manner)?

MENO: It is not.

SOCRATES: And if they administer it justly and 'prudently', will they administer it with *dikaiosune* and *sophrosune* (justice and 'prudence')?

MENO: It is inevitable.

SOCRATES: Men and women alike, then, need the same qualities if they are to be *agathoi*: *dikaiosune* and *sophrosune*.

MENO: Apparently.

Here, *dikaiosune* is the quality of co-operating fairly.[1] The interest of the passage, when taken in conjunction with the others quoted, is that it shows the relationship between *arete* and the co-operative excellences in the mind of the 'Greek in

---

[1] This is not always the case. Polemarchus in Plato's *Republic* (332A ff.) holds that it is *dikaion* to help one's *philoi* and harm one's *echthroi*; and he is speaking as an 'ordinary Greek', and referring to friends and enemies within the city. This *dikaiosune* is of course not to be equated with the *dikaiosune* of equals before the law; it is the *dikaiosune* of one who sets matters right with his own strong right arm, in the manner of Heracles; and it emphasises not co-operation but competition. This *dikaiosune* can readily be regarded as an *arete*, and as a Heraclean quality is characteristically so regarded. (Helping one's *philoi* against *echthroi* is always a mark of *arete*.)

the street' at this period. That Meno's goal is competitive—success, helping his friends and harming his enemies—is evident from all the passages; and *eu dioikein* means administering efficiently, not administering justly. Meno, when pressed by Socrates, is prepared to concede that in order to administer efficiently it is necessary to administer justly; but this is an experimental issue; and administering efficiently is a mark of *arete*, which demands that one helps one's friends and harms one's enemies, and obtains *agatha*, 'good things',[1] for them and for oneself. Since administering justly is merely the means to the desired end, then, at the point at which injustice became, or appeared to become, more conducive to the securing of the desired end than justice, anyone who held these values should, if he were clear-headed enough, pursue injustice rather than justice.[2] And these are the generally accepted values: the distinction between Meno and Thrasymachus lies not in the goal they propose to themselves, but in the means they believe most appropriate to securing it (and doubtless also in the degree of success that they suppose that their own *arete* would enable them to gain). Thrasymachus holds that injustice is always the best means to the end of success; Meno can be persuaded to support the co-operative excellences, but his words, taken as a whole, show that he would quickly abandon them if need be.

One displays *arete*, then, by securing the success in the city of a group smaller than the whole citizen-body: *arete* remains disruptive in domestic politics.

G. *Arete* and Foreign Policy

We must now consider Athens' relations with her empire. Thucydides portrays both Pericles' and Cleon's views on the subject. In Pericles' last speech, when the Athenians, ravaged by plague, are wavering in their will to fight, he says (II, 63, 2):

It is no longer possible for you to abdicate from your ruling position—supposing that anyone at this time out of

[1] And *kala*; but *kalon* simply commends the goals which the *agathos* proposes to himself, *qua agathos*, as a manifestation of his *arete*.

[2] Compare *Crito*, another 'ordinary Greek' in Plato, *Crito* 45C5 ff., discussed in *Merit and Responsibility*, pp. 230 f.

fear wishes to *apragmosunēi andragathizesthai* (play the *agathos* by remaining inactive). You hold your empire in the guise of a tyranny, which it may be *adikon* (unjust) to have taken, but is dangerous to relinquish.

Three years later Cleon says of the revolted and now defeated Mytileneans (III, 40, 4):

> In short, if you take my advice you will be inflicting a just punishment on the Mytileneans and doing *ta sumphora* (what is advantageous) for yourselves; whereas if you decide otherwise you will not please the Mytileneans, but will rather be punishing yourselves. For if they were right to revolt, then you ought not to have your empire. But if you, whether or not you should, nevertheless see fit to rule, then these men too must be punished, against equity but advantageously to yourselves, or you must abandon your empire and *andragathizesthai* (play the *agathos*) without danger.

Thucydides has a very different estimation of Pericles and Cleon; but their values, as portrayed here, are the same. They reject an *arete* which is marked by the refusal of unjust gain and an unwillingness to rule over other cities. Now the other Thucydides, son of Melesias, an oligarch and 'leader of the rich', had opposed Athens' expansionism until he was ostracised in 443 or 442; and the Corinthians, in the passage already discussed, I, 37, 5, argued that the Corcyreans could best display their *arete* by being just. This *arete* is new, opposed to traditional *arete*, which may demand a very different kind of action; and we can see how little chance it has of influencing action when faced with the demands of traditional *arete*, whether in foreign policy or any other sphere of action; for it is on the requirements of traditional *arete* that Pericles and Cleon take their stand. Traditional *arete* requires that one shall be willing to take risks to secure and increase the prosperity of the group to which one belongs: it is sharply opposed to quietism and inactivity. To juxtapose the idea of *arete* with that of inactivity or avoidance of danger is to produce, in terms of traditional *arete*, an outrageous oxymoron and to pour scorn on the new *arete*, which requires just co-operation (represented by Pericles and Cleon as mere shirking and inactivity), with a rhetoric which it could have little chance of withstanding. Traditional *arete* was far more deeply rooted, more evidently advantageous, and indeed vitally necessary in defence against the attacks of others. Small wonder that the majority of Athenians favoured her expansionism. The policy might well be even more attractive to a *kakos*, who had no personal *arete*, but might thus feel himself to be participating in the *arete* of his city, and even playing a small part in expressing it in action.

Arete is concerned with securing the well-being of one's own group: others are merely means to this end. Athens' relations with other states are illustrated by the speeches of Cleon and Diodotus in the third book of Thucydides. The Athenians were debating the appropriate treatment for the revolted and now defeated Mytilene, one of the most powerful city-states in the empire. Cleon lays great emphasis on the *adikia* of the Mytileneans, and asks for extreme penalties; but the Mytileneans' injustice is not the fundamental point of his argument. He says that he has always held that a democracy is unable to govern: a most powerful insult, for to say this is to impugn its *arete*, the *arete* of Athens.[1] Cleon wishes (38) to teach Athens' subjects a vigorous lesson by utterly destroying Mytilene; and holds that anyone who supports any other view will have to show that the *adikia* of the Mytileneans was beneficial for the Athenians, while the Athenians' misfortune had in fact harmed the Mytileneans: the irony of which requires no underlining. Diodotus speaks for clemency, but certainly not from altruistic motives (46, 4):

> And so we ought not to be precise judges of those who *exhamartanein* ('err')—and harm ourselves thereby—but rather see to it that, by punishing moderately, we retain the cities prosperous for our use, and resolve to guard ourselves not by means of the terror produced by the *nomoi*, but by the attention we pay to events.

Cleon holds that the treatment of the Mytileneans which will

[1] For *arete* as the quality that enables one to govern others, see pp. 131 f. above.

be most beneficial for Athens is what he regards as strict justice: 'if you take my advice you will treat the Mytileneans in a manner which is both just and beneficial to yourselves' (40). Diodotus believes that Athenian advantage and strict justice are opposed, and so commends the Athenians to pursue self-interest. For both, the advantage of Athens is the end, to which the Mytileneans and the rest of Athens' allies and subjects stand as means.

By 416 the Athenians, as portrayed by Thucydides, had advanced further in the ruthless application of these principles. In that year the Athenians attacked the small island of Melos, whose inhabitants, being Dorians, had not sided with the Athenians, but had not supported the Peloponnesian cause either.

They thus explain their position to the Melians (V, 89):

We ourselves will not make a long speech using fine words which would not be believed—saying either that we hold our empire *dikaiōs* (justly) because we conquered the Persians, or that we are now attacking you because we have *adikeisthai* (suffered injustice at your hands); and we advise you not to expect to persuade us by saying either that, though you are colonists of the Lacedaemonians, you have not joined with them in attacking us or that you have not *adikein* (committed injustice) against us. . . . You know as well as we do that justice . . . is the criterion when an equal necessity restrains each agent or group; but that those who are stronger do what they have the power to do, while the weak acquiesce in their actions.

Arguments based on justice are irrelevant, say the Athenians, where a powerful state's desires conflict with those of a weaker. The Melians say in reply (90) that, though they are debarred from advocating a course of action because it is just, nevertheless justice and equity are the most useful and *beneficial* courses for all to pursue: it is in one's interest to be just to the weaker, because one day one may be oneself in the weaker position. The Athenians reply (91) that they are not afraid of suffering a like fate at the hand of the Spartans, should the Spartans defeat them; for the Spartans too have subjects, and such people are not harsh to the defeated.

But we shall demonstrate that we are here to benefit our own empire, and that we are now going to make a speech designed to preserve your city; for we wish to rule over you without effort to ourselves, and you to be safe in a manner which is beneficial to both of us.

The Melians not unreasonably inquire how it would be beneficial, *chresimon*, for *them* to be enslaved, as it would be beneficial for the Athenians to rule them; and the Athenians reply that the Melians would benefit from not being destroyed, while the Athenians themselves would benefit from having the Melians as their subjects.

The Melians then state the core of their position, in terms of traditional Greek values, the values that are so closely linked to the survival of a city-state (100):

Surely, then, if you make such desperate ventures to avoid losing your empire, and those who already *douleuesthai* (are enslaved) make them to be free of their slavery, then it were a sign of great *kakotes* and *deilia* (cowardice) on the part of us who are still *eleutheroi* (free) not to make every effort to avoid our own enslavement.

The Athenians reply (101):

Not so, at all events if you consider the manner *sophronōs* ('prudently'); for the contest which you have with us is not one of *andragathia* on equal terms, (when your purpose might be) to avoid the imputation of *aischune* (disgrace). Your deliberations should be concerned rather with your safety, and you should avoid conflict with those who are much stronger than you are.

The Athenians also claim (105) that they are only acting as the Melians would act towards them if they had the chance; that a necessary *phusis* evidently leads men, and is believed to lead gods, to rule over whatever they surpass in power; and that they, the Athenians, neither established this *nomos* nor were the first to make use of it.

Sophistic thought can even enlist the claims of *phusis* to

137

maintain (105, 2) that the gods will approve the free exercise of superior power since they use the same values themselves. This rather betokens lack of belief in the gods; a believer would surely have realised that it was precisely the gods' desire to enjoy and exercise their superior *arete* that led them to regard as *hubris* any human attempt to succeed too far. But whether by absence of belief or by skilful rhetoric based on sophistic thought, fear of the gods is banished as a control; and *arete* may have free play so far as human capacity permits.

Athenian *arete*, opposed merely by a few Melians, could not be effectively restrained: the Athenians defeated the Melians, killed all the adult males, enslaved the women and children, and colonised the island themselves. It was unreasonable to expect that the Melians should successfully resist the might of Athens; and the Athenians had left little doubt of the likely fate of the defeated. Calculation of interest, then, reckoned in terms of saving their skins, might have led the Melians to submit, as the Athenians proposed; in a world of large and small cities, it was doubtless prudent that the small should defer and submit to the large; and some of Athens' subjects and allies voluntarily acted thus while Athens prospered. However, their relationship with Athens was then analogous to that of a *kakos* with the *agathoi* within his city: the Melians themselves say that submission would show them to be *kakoi* and *deiloi*, and such behaviour was unthinkable to them, for no citizen can have wished to acknowledge the *kakia* of his own city. The Melians accordingly displayed their *arete* and perished, in accordance with traditional demands, which are based not merely on avoidance of losing face, but on the facts of Greek life; defeat in battle incurs not only shame, but serious practical consequences: this is not merely a shame-culture, but also, and more fundamentally, a results-culture.

We may be tempted to say that circumstances had changed and values had not; that the Melians would have fared better by submitting, and could not have fared worse; and that, as the Athenians say themselves, values suited to the conflict of cities of comparable size are irrelevant in a conflict of the great with the small. This may be true; but the values of Athens, as we have seen in the preceding pages, give the weaker, if he submits, the status only of a useful possession to be treated or mistreated as suits the interests of the stronger. Few could relish such a status in any society; and in Greece *eleutheria*, freedom, interpreted, as we have seen, as the freedom to rule over others, was prized as highly as one might expect in a society in which slaves abounded, and ill fortune might add anyone to their number. In these circumstances, any demands that the Athenians made of the Melians or any other of their subjects would not only have imposed a burden on them in real terms; however light the burden—though there is no reason to suppose that it was, or would have been, light —it would have been bitterly resented as an abrogation of the *eleutheria* and *autarkeia*, self-sufficiency, of the subject state, and readily felt as *douleia*, slavery. True, by siding with the democrats against the *agathoi* in the cities of the empire Athens ensured their support for her, so long as they feared their own *agathoi*;[1] but once they felt themselves secure on that score, the pull of traditional *arete*—for what Greek would not have wished himself or his city to manifest *arete*?—would have ensured that the democrats resented any requirement to defer to the wishes of another city. Athens, as portrayed in the Melian Dialogue, felt free to display her *arete* as far as her powers would permit; but however she had treated them, she could never have had willing subjects: any yoke, however light, would have galled them, and once they felt able to do so, they would have wished to display their own *arete* by casting it off.

H. SOCIAL STATUS IN ATHENIAN POLITICS

In the law-courts, in internal politics and in foreign policy, competitive *arete* prevails over co-operative excellences. Other views are beginning to be expressed, but there seems little sign of their prevailing, and little likelihood that they should prevail: even when termed *arete*, the co-operative excellences are unlikely to be able to resist the pull of competitive *arete* when there is a clash between the two; for the contribution of wealth and fighting ability to the individual's, and the city's,

[1] Or, of course, the Persians; but that fear, the original cement of the League, seems to have faded by this time.

well-being is much more evident. In conclusion, we may discuss the values and likely behaviour of citizens of different classes in the politics and public life of later fifth-century Athens, a city with very democratic institutions.

It is undeniable—and I am not attempting to deny it—that Athenian direct democracy, which gave a vote to every citizen which he could exercise in person in the Assembly, put power to decide between policies laid before them into the hands of the common people of Athens to a quite unusual extent. But we sometimes tacitly assume that, because any citizen might in theory also address the Assembly, policy-making was widely spread through the citizen body. I can see little to suggest this, and much to suggest the contrary. The violence of the attacks directed at 'Cleon the tanner' readily gives a picture of an artisan snatching time from his labours to engage in politics; whereas in fact he seems to have been the son of a rich tanner, endowed with abundant leisure and the external advantages of the *agathos*—but not a member of the old political families, the old aristocracy, as were Pericles and earlier politicians. In the eyes of the common people, and in his own eyes, Cleon must have been an *agathos*; but if a Cleon, with a real basis for self-confidence in terms of much of Greek values, faced such opposition and vituperation from the established political classes and the *agathoi* authors who have come down to us, one who had not such advantages was very unlikely to open his mouth. We have seen[1] that, as represented by Thucydides, the policies and aims of Pericles and Cleon are very similar; but it seems important to Thucydides (IV, 28 ff.) that Cleon could not have had any real skill, have been, that is, *agathos* in war or politics: his failures are his own, but any success must have been the result of chance.

In the eyes of the commons, however, Cleon must have been an *agathos*. To be a 'champion of the people', of course, does not require that one is one of them: Pericles, a member of one of the noblest families in Athens, was a champion of the people; and it was for the most part such champions that the people followed and to whose policies they gave their assent. A Cleon—who may well have benefited from the new educa-

[1] Above, pp. 133 f.

tional opportunities offered by the sophists—must have been an *agathos* in the eyes of 'the many', even if he had not so many grounds for being held to be *agathos* as Pericles had.

Statements of democratic principle need very careful scrutiny in ancient Greece. Athenagoras, a Sicilian 'champion of the people' (Thucydides VI, 35) says (39):

> Someone will say that a democracy is neither *suneton* (practically wise) nor *ison* (fair), and that those who have property are also most *agathoi* at governing. But I say, first that democracy is a name for all, oligarchy for only a part, secondly that the wealthy are the most *agathoi* guardians of property, but the *sunetoi* (the practically wise) would be the best counsellors, and the *polloi* (the many), after hearing matters discussed, would be the best judges; and that these classes together *isomoirein* (have an equal share) in a democracy. An oligarchy gives a share of dangers to the *polloi*, but not only claims the larger share of benefits but even takes away and keeps everything.

Wealth, says Athenagoras, is not a sufficient criterion for being good at governing; and we may well, on reading *sunetoi*, suppose that his criterion is simply political skill and intelligence. But observe that the *polloi* who are contrasted with the rulers in an oligarchy are also those who, immediately above, are to judge and vote on the speeches of the *sunetoi*. When contrasted with the rich 'few', they are a social group; and it seems likely that the usage is the same in the sentence before. Athenagoras simply assumes that anyone who is *sunetos* in politics will not be one of the *polloi*: wealth, and the other externals commended by *arete*, are not sufficient, but they are necessary. We may compare Pericles' claim that men are advanced to public office in Athens 'from *arete*' (above, p. 105). He adds that poverty does not stand in one's way, '*at all events if one is able to benefit, agathon dran*, the city'. More may be implied by that 'at all events' than is at first sight apparent. We have observed the usage of *arete*, and the kind of *agatha* that are esteemed by the democratic juries, and render one *agathos*; and we may perhaps wonder to what extent anyone who, being unable to confer such *agatha* on the city, was not *agathos* but *kakos*, an inferior specimen of a human being, could nerve himself to address the Assembly and contend with those who were *agathoi*, good specimens of human beings. When Theseus says in the *Suppliant Women* (above, p. 104) that 'he who wishes (to speak) is famous, and he who does not wish, remains silent' the words are advertising copy for Athenian democracy seen from above, rather than a factual description: 'does not wish' for the *kakos* might well be 'is inhibited from speaking'. Euripides' account of Athenian courts in the preceding lines appears optimistic in the light of Athenian forensic speeches; and these lines too seem unlikely to accord closely with the actual situation.

Some words of Nicias may throw more light. He regarded the Sicilian expedition as rash, which might well leave him open to the charge of 'wishing to play the *agathos* without danger' (above, p. 134). He must accordingly deny that he is afraid for his own skin, claiming on the contrary (Thucydides VI, 9, 2)

> That a man who displays some forethought for his own safety and that of his property is none the less an *agathos polites*, for such a man would, in his own interest, be most anxious that the city's affairs too should prosper.

Like many generalisations in Thucydides' speeches, these words are not over-relevant to the case in hand, and may be applied more widely. They seem to indicate, from their defensive tone, that the people of Athens expected the *agathos polites* to be at all times ready to hazard his own property in the city's interest. In the law-courts, too, the *agathos* must show that he has lavished his own money and efforts on the city's behalf; and the *agathos* or *agathos polites* is of course the same person in both contexts. Furthermore, the objects on which the *agathos* is expected to disburse his money are expensive ones: there would be little point in claiming that one had expended the little one had in the city's interest.

Alcibiades adds more to the picture (Thucydides VI, 16, 1 ff.):

> It both befits me rather than others, Athenians, to govern . . . and I think too that I am worthy of it. For

those things for which I am abused bring reputation to my ancestors and myself, and benefit, in addition, to my native land. For the Greeks, who previously hoped that the city had been exhausted by the war, came to suppose it even greater than is actually the case, as a result of my display on my mission to the Olympic games, since I entered seven chariots, a number that no private individual had ever entered before, and won the first prize and the second and the fourth, and made all other arrangements in a manner worthy of my victory. For by *nomos* (convention) such things bring *time* (honour); and power too is inferred from what is done. Again, my conspicuousness in the city, whether in the furnishing of choruses or anything else, is by *phusis* the cause of *phthonos* (envy) to the citizens, but to strangers this too is a manifestation of power. And it is not *achrēstos* (useless) folly, when a man by spending his own money benefits not only himself but also his city. Nor is it *adikon* (unjust) that such a man should *mega phronein* (think big) about himself and should not be *isos* (equal) since he who fares ill *isomoirein* (shares equally) his misfortunes with no-one. No; just as we are greeted by no-one when we suffer misfortune, in the same way a man should endure being despised by those who enjoy good fortune, or let him deal equally with all men and claim the same treatment in return. But I know that such (i.e. outstanding) men, and anyone who has attained to any kind of fame, cause offence during their lifetimes, *especially to those similar to themselves*, and then to the rest, while they are still among them, but that they cause those who come after them to claim kinship with them even where no kinship exists, and occasion pride to their country, whatever it be, as men who are not foreigners nor *hamartontes* (in error) but their own citizens and men who have done *kala*.

Conspicuous expenditure devoted to winning at the Olympic games is argued to confer benefits on the city as a whole. Xenophanes had complained a century earlier[1] that such success, though useless, brought great honour. Alcibiades

[1] Above, p. 47; and cf. Euripides Nauck[2] frag. 282.

makes out a case for its usefulness; that honour is derived from it is abundantly clear; it certainly displays the *arete* of the victor, as do other, more tangible, benefits, such as the furnishing of choruses; and the fame derived can evidently, as in Alcibiades' case, be translated into political power and influence.

Note that though Alcibiades speaks of the *phthonos*, envy, of 'the citizens', he later supposes that the resentment will be most intense among 'those similar (to the successful man)'. *Arete* is still highly competitive, and the success of one, *kalon* to himself, puts others into a position that is relatively more *aischron* than it was, if they hold themselves to be *agathoi*. The *kakos* is not thrown into the shade, of course: he is there already. In the previous chapter (VI, 15, 4) Thucydides says that 'the many' became hostile to Alcibiades because they thought that he was aiming at a tyranny. Yet at the time of the mutilation of the Hermae (VI, 28), Thucydides says that those who took up the charges were those who most resented him

> Since they thought that he hindered them from being secure in their leadership of the common people, and thinking that if they drove him out they would be first. . . .

The thought of someone else becoming a tyrant over him, or of one other person increasing his powers at the expense of others in the city, is likely to be abhorrent to a Greek in proportion as he feels self-sufficient and self-reliant; and *arete* denotes and commends those characteristics which are held to conduce to self-sufficiency, *autarkeia*. So an *agathos* must have aroused *phthonos* in his fellow-*agathoi* by the self-same actions as he could mention to his great advantage were he on trial in court before a jury of *kakoi*. Tyranny—or even a position which could be plausibly represented by others as being a tyranny—would now, it might be thought, be too much for any free Athenian to stomach; and this may in fact be so. The free Athenian, after all, now had his vote, and would be likely to resent any change of constitution which deprived him of it. Yet we have seen Lysias (above, pp. 124 f.) nervous about a popular jury's attitude to Eratosthenes, one of the Thirty and an undoubted murderer, but one who could doubtless have produced a long list of *agatha* conferred. Deference still evidently had a large, if perhaps a decreasing, part to play in the attitude of the *kakos*.

In conclusion, a few words about the situation of the traditional *agathoi*, the cavalry and hoplite classes, during the Peloponnesian War. Their usual function in wars between Greek cities had been to furnish essential defence, the ground of their claim to be *agathoi*. Pericles, however, refused to lead them out against the Peloponnesian army, holding that Athens behind her walls was virtually an island, and must rely on her sea-power. This strategically justified decision left the *agathoi* without a military function (though the cavalry were given some fighting, Thucydides II, 22, 2); and if, during the war or at any other time, the common people and the 'champions of the people' favoured one policy while the *agathoi* as a group favoured another, the *agathoi* must inevitably have been outvoted. Both of these situations, as we have seen, are *aischron* and detract from the *arete* of the *agathos*. To wipe out such stains, and to benefit one's associates and harm one's enemies in the city, by just or unjust means, whichever be the more efficacious, is a demand of *arete* (above, pp. 131 ff.). Furthermore, those—of wealthy families, for reasons already stated—who wished, and were able, to benefit fully from sophistic instruction in the 'political art', but did not wish to be 'champions of the people', must have been unable to exercise effectively that superior skill that they believed themselves to possess, or to rule over others as an *agathos* should. Though the champions of the people were presumably always regarded as *agathoi* by the common people, and some of them by *agathoi* as well, the *agathoi* as a group with interests of their own were thrown into the shade. That they should try to wipe out the stain and re-establish themselves, by moderate means, as in the revolution of 411, more violently in the manner of the Thirty at the end of the Peloponnesian War, is not surprising, for it was enjoined upon them by the most powerful values of ancient Greece, which not only lead to civil war but enjoin it on any individual or group which, regarding itself as *agathos*, is consistently worsted.

In both foreign and domestic politics, then, it was essential for any individual or state that claimed to be *agathos* not to submit to any situation which entailed, or appeared to entail, defeat, reduction of *eleutheria*, freedom, or *autarkeia*, self-sufficiency; for any such situation reduced or abolished one's *arete*, the most important quality. One might have to bide one's time; but so soon as an opportunity offered, the most powerful values of the society demanded that one should worst one's enemies, within or without the city, whatever the rights and wrongs of the case reckoned in terms of *dikaiosune*. Athens' hold over her empire must always have been uneasy; and the cause of the frequency of *stasis*, civil strife, in Greek cities is not far to seek. While the independent city-state was held to be the best form of political unit, these values were naturally cherished in relationships between city-states; but it was of the utmost importance, in the interests of the continued existence and well-being of the city-state, that its members should value co-operative justice in their relationships with each other more highly than maximising their own success by any efficient means, unjust or no. Now had the Greeks of the period recognised the importance to the well-being of the city-state of the co-operative excellences, they should have rated them as *aretai* along with the traditional ones. In the earlier part of this chapter we observed a number of insights and aspirations: insight into the importance of co-operative excellences was expressed by several writers with intellectual 'sophistic' interests, in contexts where practical, real-life decisions were for the most part not at issue. We have also seen, however, evident and urgent practical needs of the city-state which rendered it unlikely that most citizens would attain to such insights,[1] much less act upon them: other qualities seemed to contribute so much more to the desired end. The insights needed are political: it is not that the Greeks have abandoned traditional values to which they might be recalled by moral suasion or

[1] They were attained once or twice in the law-courts, Lysias 18. 17; 21. 19; 26. 4; for which see *Merit and Responsibility* pp. 210 ff. What is required, however, is a general realisation of what is needed accompanied by a thorough adjustment of values such as only a major moral and political philosopher is likely to achieve.

rhetoric, but that they have retained their traditional values in a situation far different from that in which the values had developed and to which they were appropriate. After the political upheavals at Athens in the closing years of the Peloponnesian War, no Greek could overlook the existence of the problem, even if he could neither formulate it clearly to himself nor suggest a solution. A Plato or an Aristotle was needed; and their solutions are naturally given shape by the characteristics of the problem; but this question lies beyond the scope of the present book.[1]

---

[1] See, however, *Merit and Responsibility*, chapters xii–xvi, *From the Many to the One*, chapters vi and vii.

Select Bibliography

I Sources: Texts And Translations

My translations are for the most part based on the 'Oxford Classical Text' (Scriptorum Classicorum Bibliotheca Oxoniensis, Clarendon Press, Oxford), where such exists, of the author concerned. Lyric and elegiac poems are cited with the numbering of the Loeb Classical Library, and the translation is based on the text printed there, since that series provides the texts of those authors most likely to be available to those who are not professional scholars. (I have taken care to ensure that using these texts results in no important differences of interpretation.) The translation of the fragments of 'Pre-Socratics' is based on the text of *Die Fragmente der Vorsokratiker*, 3 vols., edited by H. Diels and W. Kranz (6th edition, Berlin, Weidmannsche Verlagsbuchhandlung, 1951–2). There is an English translation of the 'B' passages—the fragments held to be authentic—from Diels/Kranz in K. Freeman, *Ancilla to the Presocratic Philosophers* (Oxford, Blackwell, Cambridge, Mass., Harvard University Press, 1948). There are numerous translations of most of the authors discussed in this work. The Greekless reader desirous of pursuing further for himself the questions I have raised would be well advised to learn at least the Greek alphabet—a task whose difficulty is frequently exaggerated by those who have not attempted it—and then consult the translations of the Loeb Classical Library, where a page of English is faced by the original Greek, so that he may ascertain whether a particular Greek word was or was not used by the author he is studying. But it is always better to consult several translations of the same passage: it is not only the words discussed in this book that pose difficulties of translation, and the idiom of any one translator may suggest ideas and overtones that are not present in the original. ('Penguin' translations are inexpensive and readily obtainable, and for the most part useful; but I do not recommend the 'Penguin' *Iliad* and *Odyssey* to those who wish to pursue the questions discussed in this book.)

II Secondary Material

A. *Semantics, Meaning and Values*. A few important works in English on this very large subject must suffice:

R. M. Hare, *The Language of Morals* (Oxford, Clarendon Press, 1952; New York, Oxford University Press, 1964).

C. K. Ogden, and I. A. Richards, *The Meaning of Meaning; a Study of the Influence of Language upon Thought and the Science of Symbolism* (London, Kegan Paul; New York, Harcourt Brace, 1923).

C. S. Stevenson, *Ethics and Language* (New Haven, Yale University Press, 1944).

L. Wittgenstein, *Philosophical Investigations* (tr. by G. E. M. Anscombe, Oxford, Blackwell, 1953; New York, Barnes & Noble, 1969).

B. *General.* This section contains a selection of works whose themes range beyond those of the individual chapters of this book.

A. W. H. Adkins, *Merit and Responsibility; a Study in Greek Values* (Oxford, Clarendon Press; New York, Oxford University Press, 1960) This work continues the discussion of some of the questions raised in the present book as far as Aristotle, and contains references to more passages of Greek authors from Homer to the end of the fifth century than are discussed here.

—— *From the Many to the One; a Study of Personality and Views of Human Nature in the Context of Ancient Greek Society, Values and Beliefs* (London, Constable, and Ithaca, New York, Cornell University Press, 1970). This work discusses Greek values from Homer to Epicurus, and endeavours to trace connections between values and certain psychological phenomena observable in Greek literature. It contains a larger bibliography than I have been able to include here.

A. Andrewes, *The Greeks* (London, Hutchinson; New York, Alfred A. Knopf, 1967).

H. C. Baldry, *The Unity of Mankind in Greek Thought* (Cambridge and New York, Cambridge University Press, 1965).

E. R. Dodds, *The Greeks and the Irrational* (Berkeley and Los Angeles, University of California Press, 1951).

W. G. Forrest, *The Emergence of Greek Democracy* (London, Weidenfeld and Nicolson, 1966).

SELECT BIBLIOGRAPHY

G. Glotz, *The Greek City and its Institutions* (London, Kegan Paul, 1929; New York, Barnes & Noble, 1965).

A. W. Gouldner, *Enter Plato* (New York, Basic Books, 1965). The first part of this work is devoted to Greek thought and attitudes before Plato. The work as a whole is a sociological analysis of Greek values and society.

W. Jaeger, *Paideia* (tr. by G. Highet, 3 vols., Oxford, Blackwell, 1939–45; New York, Oxford University Press, 1965).

H. D. F. Kitto, *The Greeks* (Harmondsworth, Penguin, 1951).

B. Snell, *The Discovery of the Mind* (tr. by T. G. Rosenmeyer, Oxford, Blackwell, 1953; New York, Harper Row).

C. *The Homeric Poems.*

A. W. H. Adkins, ' "Honour" and "Punishment" in the Homeric Poems', *Bulletin of the Institute of Classical Studies* vii (1960), 23 ff.; ' "Friendship" and "Self-Sufficiency" in Homer and Aristotle', *Classical Quarterly* n.s. xiii (1963), 30 ff.; '*Euchomai, euchōlē* and *euchos* in Homer', *Classical Quarterly* n.s. xix (1969), 20 ff.; 'Threatening, Abusing and feeling Angry in the Homeric Poems', *Journal of Hellenic Studies* lxxxix (1969) 7 ff.; and 'Homeric values and Homeric Society', *Journal of Hellenic Studies* xci (1971) 1 ff. These articles contain studies in Homeric society, values and psychology; the last is a reply to A. A. Long, 'Morals and Values in Homer', *Journal of Hellenic Studies* xc (1970), 121 ff.

C. M. Bowra, *Tradition and Design in the Iliad* (Oxford, Clarendon Press, 1930).

M. I. Finley, *The World of Odysseus* (London, Chatto and Windus, 1956; New York, Viking Press, 1965).

—— *Early Greece: The Bronze and Archaic Ages* (London, Chatto and Windus, 1970; New York, W. W. Norton and Co. Inc., 1970).

G. S. Kirk, *The Songs of Homer* (Cambridge and New York, Cambridge University Press, 1962).

A. B. Lord, *The Singer of Tales* (Cambridge, Mass., Harvard University Press, 1960).

A. J. B. Wace, and F. H. Stubbings, *A Companion to Homer* (London, Macmillan, 1962; New York, 1963).

T. B. L. Webster, *From Mycenae to Homer* (2nd edn., London, Methuen, 1964; New York, W. W. Norton & Co. Inc., 1964).

D. *From Hesiod to the Sixth Century.*

A. Andrewes, *The Greek Tyrants* (London, Hutchinson, 1956; New York, Harper and Row).

C. M. Bowra, Greek Lyric Poetry from Aleman to Simonides (2nd. rev. edn., Oxford, Clarendon Press, and New York, Oxford University Press 1961).

A. R. Burn, *The Lyric Age of Greece* (London, Arnold, 1960; New York, Funk & Wagnalls).

K. Freeman, *The Life Work of Solon*; with a Translation of his Poems (Cardiff, University of Wales Press, and London, Oxford University Press, 1926).

I. M. Linforth, *Solon the Athenian* (Berkeley, University of California Press, 1919).

F. Solmsen, *Hesiod and Aeschylus* (Ithaca, Cornell University Press, 1949).

P N. Ure, *The Origin of Tyranny* (Cambridge, Cambridge University Press, 1922; New York, Russell (Atheneum) 1962).

W. J. Woodhouse, *Solon the Liberator* (London, Oxford University Press 1938; New York, Octagon, Farrar, Straus & Giroux, 1965).

E. *The Earlier Fifth Century.*

J. H. Finley, jnr., *Pindar and Aeschylus* (Cambridge, Mass., Harvard University Press, 1955).

G. M. Kirkwood, *A Study of Sophoclean Drama* (Ithaca, Cornell University Press, 1958).

H. D. F. Kitto, *Sophocles, Dramatist and Philosopher* (London, Oxford University Press, 1958).

SELECT BIBLIOGRAPHY

Sir John Myres, *Herodotus, Father of History* (Oxford, Clarendon Press, 1953; New York, Oxford University Press).

G. Norwood, *Pindar* (Berkeley, University of California Press, 1945).

J. C. Opstelten, *Sophocles and Greek Pessimism* (tr. by J. A. Ross, Amsterdam, North-Holland Publishing Company, 1952).

J. E. Powell, *The History of Herodotus* (Cambridge, Cambridge University Press, 1939).

G. D. Thomson, *Aeschylus and Athens; a Study in the Social Origins of Greek Drama* (2nd edn., London, Lawrence and Wishart, 1946; New York, Haskell, 1969).

T. B. L. Webster, *An Introduction to Sophocles* (Oxford, Clarendon Press, 1936).

F. *The Later Fifth Century.*

F. M. Cornford, *From Religion to Philosophy* (London, Arnold, 1912; Lexington, Mass., Peter Smith, 1958).

—— *Before and after Socrates* (Cambridge, Cambridge University Press, 1932).

K. J. Dover, *Lysias and the Corpus Lysiacum* (Berkeley, University of California Press, 1968).

J. H. Finley, jnr., *Thucydides* (Cambridge, Mass., Harvard University Press, 1942).

J. Gould, *The Development of Plato's Ethics* (Cambridge, Cambridge University Press, 1955).

G. M. A. Grube, *The Drama of Euripides* (London, Methuen, 1941).

——*Plato's Thought* (London, Methuen, 1935; Boston, Mass., Beacon Press, 1958).

G. B. Grundy, *Thucydides and the History of his Age* (2nd edn., Oxford, Clarendon Press, 1948).

W. K. C. Guthrie, *A History of Greek Philosophy*, Vol. III (Cambridge, Cambridge University Press, 1969).

W. H. S. Jones, *Philosophy and Medicine in Ancient Greece* (Baltimore, Johns Hopkins Press, 1946).

G. S. Kirk and J. E. Raven, *The Presocratic Philosophers, a Critical History with a Selection of Texts* (2nd edn., Cambridge, Cambridge University Press, 1960).

M. J. O'Brien, *The Socratic Paradoxes and the Greek Mind* (Chapel Hill, University of North Carolina Press, 1967).

A. E. Taylor, *Plato: the Man and his Work* (London, Methuen, 1926).

The standard one-volume histories of the period available in English are:

J. B. Bury, *A History of Greece to the Death of Alexander the Great* (3rd edn., revised by R. Meiggs, London, Macmillan, 1951; New York, St. Martin's Press, 1951).

N. G. L. Hammond, *A History of Greece to 322 B.C.* (Oxford, Clarendon Press, 1959; New York, Oxford University Press, 1967).

Longer (and older) is

The Cambridge Ancient History (edited by J. B. Bury, S. A. Cook and F. E. Adcock, M. P. Charlesworth and N. H. Baynes, Cambridge, Cambridge University Press, 1926 to 1939).

Volumes iv and v are relevant to the period of this work.

INDEX

Achilles, 11, 13, 14 f., 21
Adikein, 103, 122, 136
Adikiā, 73, 74 f., 92, 118 f., 135 f.
Adikon, -a, 113, 134, 143
Adikos, -oi, 32, 48
Administration, 111, 117, 132 f.
Aeschines, 124
Aeschylus, 59 f., 78, 85 f., 88 ff.,
    92 ff., 96 ff., 100 ff., 113 f., 115
Agamemnon, 11, 13, 14, 21, 89
Agathon, -a, 25, 28, 35 ff., 45, 52,
    55, 69, 78, 79 ff., 101, 104 f.,
    122 ff., 131, 141
Agathos, -oi, in Homer, Chapter
    2 *passim*; in Hesiod, 23 ff.,; in
    Tyrtaeus, 35 ff.; in Theognis,
    37 ff.; in Solon, 47 ff.; in the
    earlier fifth century, 60 ff., 65 ff.,
    68 ff., 73 ff., 76 ff., 79 ff., 85 ff.,
    90, 93 ff., 97 ff.; in the later
    fifth century, 99, 102, 108 ff.,
    112 ff., 115 ff., 119 ff., 126 ff.,
    131, 133 ff., 137 ff., 139 ff.,
    145 ff.
Agathos polītēs, -oi . . . -ai, 111 f.,
    124, 126 ff., 142
Agorā, 24, 91
Aidōs, 18 f., 25 f., 32, 104, 128
Aisa, see Moira
Aischron, -a, 12 ff., 26, 31, 55 f.,
    60 f., 70 f., 107, 109, 113 ff.
Aischūnein, 34, 36, 55
Alcibiades, 77, 142 ff.
Alcinous, 15
Amēchaniā, 45 f., 62, 71 f., 101
Amphiaraus, 94
Andragathizesthai, 134
Animals, 30 f.

Antigone, 86, 88, 114, 127
Antiphon the Sophist, 107 f., 110
Archidamus, King of Sparta,
    128 f.
Aretē, -ai, 6 f.; in Homer, 12 ff.,
    18 ff., 22; in Hesiod, 25 ff.,
    30, 32 ff.; in Tyrtaeus, 35 ff.;
    in Theognis, 37 ff., 42 f., 45 f.;
    in Solon, 55 f.; in the earlier
    fifth century, 58, 60 ff., 75,
    76 ff., 87, 90, 93 ff.; in the
    later fifth century, 99, 102, 103,
    105, 108 ff., 112 ff., 115 ff.,
    117, 118 f., 119 ff., 122, 126 ff.,
    133 ff., 137 ff., 139 ff., 145 ff.
Aristophanes, 40
Aristotle, 42, 43, 50, 120, 147
Art, *see Technē*
Assembly, 11 f., 22, 40, 65, 104 f.,
    111 f., 120, 124, 128, 130 f.,
    140, 142
Ātē, -ai, 27 ff., 48, 53, 85
Athena, 48
Athens, 47 ff., 54, 59, 63, 64 f.,
    93 ff., 100, 112, 119 ff., 128 f.,
    133 ff., 139 ff., 144, 145 ff.
Atīmiā, 36, 91
Autarkeia, 139, 144, 146

Bacchylides, 59, 62 f., 67, 82, 95
Barbarians, 58 f.
Beggars, 20, 29, 33 f.
Benefit, *see Agathon, -a*
'Birth', 13, 38 ff., 64, 74, 108, 122,
    140, 142 f.; and *see Phusis*
Bonner and Smith, 126

Callicles, 109 ff., 113

155

INDEX

Caprice, of gods, 45, 81 f.
Carpenters, 33
Cavalry, 61, 116, 145
'Champions of the people', 140 f., 145
Chrēstos, -oi, 63; and see *Agathos*
Civil Strife, see *Stasis*
Cleobis and Bito, 79 ff.
Cleon, 64 f., 110, 124, 128 f., 133 ff., 140
Clever, see *Deinos*, *Sophos*
Clytemnestra, 86, 89
Comer, see *Hiketēs*
Conflict, see *Dēris*
Conscience, 81
Co-operation, 15 ff., 27, 132, 134 f.
Courage, 13; and see *Agathos*, *Aretē*
Creon, 86 f., 127 ff.
Critias, 102, 108, 118
Crito, 133
Croesus, 43, 79 ff.
Custom, see *Nomos*
Cyrnus, 38 ff.

Deference, 13 f., 64 ff., 125
Deilos, -oi, 12 ff., 27 f., 39, 62
Deinon, -a, 92, 100 f.
Deioces, 71
Delphi, 79, 82 f.
Democracy, 65, 67, 71, 74, 104 ff. 120 ff., 130, 140 ff.
Democritus, 97, 103, 107
Demosthenes, 121
Denniston, J. D., 116
Dēris, 32 ff.
Dikaios, -oi, 20, 32, 42, 73, 88, 90 ff., 123 f., 127
Dikaiosunē, 42 f., 74, 85, 90, 93 f., 107, 117 ff., 124, 132, 136, 146; and see also *Dikē*
Dikē, -ai, 31, 84, 90 ff., 102 f.; and see also *Dikaiosunē*

156

Diodotus, 135 f.
Dusnomiā, 48 ff., 56

Echthros, -oi, 52, 55 f., 61, 131 ff., 145
Electra, 86, 88, 89
Elencheiē, 12 ff.
Eleutheriā, 68 f., 104, 112, 119, 129 f., 137 ff., 139, 146
Enemy (within the city), see *Echthros*
Envy, see *Phthonos*
Equality, 68, 92, 104 f., 114
Erinyes, 90 ff., 96, 101
Esthlos, see *Agathos*
Eubouliā, 111, 127, 128 f.
Eudaimōn, 45, 75, 77 ff.
Eudaimoniā, 75, 77 ff.
Eunomiā, 46 ff., 56, 84 f.
Euripides, 75, 83, 102, 104 ff., 114 ff., 120, 143
Eusebeia, 82
Eusebēs, 83
Eutuchein, 104
Excellences, Competitive, 9, 14 ff., 33, 43, 67, 70, 77, 80, 85, 95, 99, 112, 139, 146
Excellences, Co-operative, 9, 14 ff., 31 f., 43 f., 77, 92 ff., 98, 114, 116, 118, 127, 133, 139, 146

Family, 91 f., 112, 115 f., 122; and see *Oikos*
Finley, M. I., 11, 16
Folk-tales, 26, 81
Folly, see *Ātē*
Freedom, see *Eleutheriā*
Friendship, see *Philotēs*, *Philiā*
Furies, see *Erinyes*

Games, 47, 59, 62 ff., 75 f., 79, 142 ff.

INDEX

Gentlemen, 117, 126; and see
  Kalos kāgathos
Gods, in Homer, 17, 19 f.; in
  Hesiod, 27 ff.; in Theognis, 38,
  43 ff.; in Solon, 48 f., 53; in
  the earlier fifth century, 60 f.,
  62, 75, 78 ff., 82 ff., 87 ff.,
  92 ff., 99 ff.; in the later fifth
  century, 100 ff., 118, 137 f.
Gomme, A. W., 105
Gorgias, 111
Gratitude, of gods, 82
Guest-friendship, see Xeniē, Xeinos
Gyges, 82

Hades, 20, 78, 95 ff.
Hamartiā aischrā, 115
Hare, R. M., 6
Harm, see Kakon
Hawk, and Nightingale, 30 f.
Hellenes, 58 f.
Heracles, and justice, 114
Herodotus, the historian, 59, 61,
  68 f., 71, 73 f., 77 f., 82, 86, 93,
  100, 107, 116, 130 f.
Herodotus of Thebes, 76
Hesiod, 23 ff., 45, 53 f., 57
Hiero of Syracuse, 68, 72, 82 f.,
  114
Hiketēs, -ai, 17, 20, 27
Homer, 1, Chapter 2 passim, 22 f.,
  35, 38 f., 42 f., 45, 63, 78, 82,
  106
Honesty, 7
Honour, see Tiein, Tīmān, Tīmē
Hoplites, 37, 40, 61 f., 119, 123,
  145
Hosion, -a, 82, 113
Household, 117 ff., 132; and see
  Oikos
Hubris, 27 ff., 44 f., 48, 51 ff., 69 f.,
  84 ff., 99, 102, 138; and Justice,
  87 ff.

Hymn to Demeter, 95 f.

'Immoralists', 109, 113, 119
Immortality, 20, 36, 95 ff.
Initiation, 95 ff.
Injustice, 21, 27 ff., 37, 43 ff., 48,
  51 f., 53 ff., 70, 73 ff., 75 ff.,
  78 ff., 99, 101, 118, 124, 133,
  136 ff.; and Hubris, 88; and
  see Adikiā
Intentions, 13 ff., 17, 19 f.
Isomoiriā, 50
Ison, -a, 104 ff., 141, 143
Isonomiā, 73 f.

Jebb, R. C., 129
Johnson, S., 33
Juries, 72, 102 ff.
Justice, 8; in Homer, 20 f.; in
  Hesiod, 27 ff.; in Theognis,
  42 ff.; in Solon, 48, 52 ff.; in
  the earlier fifth century, 71 f.,
  78 ff., 83 ff., 92 ff., 99; in the
  later fifth century, 101, 103 ff.,
  107 ff., 111 f., 118 f., 121 ff.,
  133, 136 ff.; and Heracles, 114;
  and Hubris, 87 ff.; and Moira,
  90 ff.; and see Dikaios, Dikaiosunē

Kakiā, 34
Kakon, -a, 27, 32, 36, 44 f., 48,
  52, 80, 101, 109, 115
Kakos, -oi, in Homer, 12 ff., 22;
  in Hesiod, 26 f., 29 f., 32; in
  Tyrtaeus, 35; in Theognis,
  37 ff.; in Solon, 50, 52, 54; in
  the earlier fifth century, 60 ff.,
  73 f., 76, 90, 99; in the later
  fifth century, 102, 113, 120,
  128 ff., 135, 137 ff.
Kakotēs, 12 ff., 25, 35 f., 69, 116,
  137; and see also Kakiā

INDEX

INDEX

INDEX

Wealth, 13, 23, 35, 38 ff., 49, 52 ff., 62 ff., 79 ff., 83, 112, 119 ff., 141 f.

Weapons, 13, 16, 37, 39, 61 f., 66, 123 f.

Wise, *see Sophos, Sunetos*

Work, 25, 32 f.

Xeinos, -oi, 17 f., 20, 94

Xeniē, 16

Xenocrates of Acragas, 76 f.

Xenophanes, 47, 143

Xenophon, 126, 131

Zeus, 17, 20, 27 ff., 38, 48, 60, 82, 84, 88, 91, 105, 113; 'another Zeus', i.e. Hades, 96 f.